MAKING SENSE *of* MINDFULNESS

MAKING
SENSE *of*
MINDFULNESS

*Five Principals to Integrate Mindfulness
Practice into Your Daily Life*

Keith Macpherson

NEW YORK

LONDON • NASHVILLE • MELBOURNE • VANCOUVER

MAKING SENSE *of* MINDFULNESS
Five Principals to Integrate Mindfulness Practice into Your Daily Life

Published in New York, New York, by Morgan James Publishing. Morgan James is a trademark of Morgan James, LLC. www.MorganJamesPublishing.com

The Morgan James Speakers Group can bring authors to your live event. For more information or to book an event visit The Morgan James Speakers Group at www.TheMorganJamesSpeakersGroup.com.

ISBN 978-1-68350-952-3 paperback
ISBN 978-1-68350-953-0 eBook
Library of Congress Control Number: 2018901062

Cover Design by:
Rachel Lopez
www.r2cdesign.com

Interior Design by:
Bonnie Bushman
The Whole Caboodle Graphic Design

In an effort to support local communities, raise awareness and funds, Morgan James Publishing donates a percentage of all book sales for the life of each book to Habitat for Humanity Peninsula and Greater Williamsburg.

Get involved today! Visit
www.MorganJamesBuilds.com

Dedicated to Dr. Wayne Dyer and Louise L. Hay,
two luminous beings who deeply affected my life.

CONTENTS

ACKNOWLEDGEMENTS

In addition to dedicating this book to my mentors, Dr. Wayne Dyer and Louise L. Hay, I would like to honor the many people who supported me and inspired me in writing these pages. First and foremost, I want to thank my wife, Kristen, for being such an incredible light in my life. You continue to inspire me and motivate me to be the best I can be. I also would like to thank my family for their unconditional support and encouragement as I continue to push my edges and test the waters. Mom and Dad, Kyle, Darcy, the Ollinger family, and Mark Reeves, thank you! Thank you to my manager and dear friend, Robyn Braha, for your ongoing support and belief in the work which we offer the planet together. I would also like to "love on" my dear friend and mentor, Dave Jaworski, for believing in me and my vision. You have a very special place in my heart. Thank you to Janice Filmon and Gary Filmon who have been such incredible mentors and friends of mine and have always encouraged me to pursue my dreams. Thank you to Karen Kimsey-

House and Henry Kimsey-House for teaching me about how to live co-actively in this world.

The five-step framework in this book developed over several years of self-study and inspiration, and I put it together by combining many resources that have deeply affected my life. I would like to honor Catherine Eby, Clive Prout, the Coaching Training Institute (CTI), Catherine Ponder, Florence Shinn, New Heights Camp, Dr. Serge King, the University of Winnipeg's Faculty of Education, Jennifer Dyck, Brad Nance, Garth Collier, Irina Volchok, and all the other friends who supported me on this journey, offering inspiration and guidance.

Finally, I would like to thank my publisher, Morgan James Publishing, for assisting me with bringing this important message into the world. I am truly grateful for your partnership and look forward to many years of working together.

PREFACE

To begin anything new requires letting go of the old. To begin this book, I must let go of my doubts and fears about whether or not the right words will be written. I must let go of my procrastination and excuses for why this project must be put on the back-burner. I also must let go of my worries about what other people might think about this body of work.

I sit here in my meditation space in Winnipeg, Manitoba, Canada. It's early in the morning, and a candle is lit. I am writing these words onto page number one in my red scribbler. It has been a long time coming, and I have finally mustered up the courage to fully immerse myself in the writing of this book. For the last four years, whenever people ask me what I have been up to, one of my immediate answers has been, "I am writing a book." It is only today, however, that I am fully committing to this journey. The thought of writing this book has been like a seed growing in my imagination for quite some time.

As I sit here in this very moment, the words are gradually flowing out onto the page and, ultimately, out into the universe. I can no longer deny this journey I am on. This has been a very long time coming, and the time has finally arrived. Through the writing of this book, it's my hope that what I channel onto these pages will arrive at the perfect time for you. I believe everything shows up in our lives at the perfect time to support us on our journey—there are no accidents.

So, in the attempt to write and finish this book, I am publicly committing to let go of my fear and hesitation so that new wisdom and inspiration can flow through me to you. It's my dream that the words of this book will inspire you to live more mindfully and to consider consciously taking the next step toward the authentic dream forming in your own imagination. As Victor Hugo so powerfully writes, "There is nothing more powerful than an idea whose time has come." It is time.

Love,

Keith

INTRODUCTION

Over the past few years the word "mindful" has become quite a buzz word in our culture. It has often been associated with the practice of slowing down our thoughts and paying more attention to the present moment. Although this word is used frequently in our culture, very few understand the depth of what "mindfulness" actually means or how to integrate this concept into everyday life. So, what has triggered such interest in this word as of late, and why are there so many different interpretations of its meaning?

We live in a world of "busyness," a world of noise and constant coming and going. The increased use of technology and its offshoots, including social media, text messaging, and email—all of which, ironically, were designed to connect us to the world—has ultimately disconnected us from the present moment. We find ourselves habitually checking our handheld devices for the latest updates and unconsciously sacrificing opportunities to be present with the life that surrounds us.

We may even find ourselves avoiding in-person conversations for a few extra minutes of screen time. In addition, our culture has become increasingly fast-paced and driven to acquire more, be more, and do more. As we hurry off to the next task at hand, not much time is left to process and feel our emotions in the present. We are a culture of multitaskers programmed to believe that the more items we check off our to-do lists, the further ahead we will get. The question is, where exactly are we rushing to get to anyway? What drives us to be outside of the moment we are currently experiencing?

Our generation has more anxiety, depression, and stress than ever before recorded. Families and individuals all around the world are struggling to find the peace and connection that past generations were accustomed to. We have come to a tipping point in our current world, and it seems many of us are trying to find a way back to the secrets of inner peace, simplicity, and connection.

Over the past eight years, I have studied, experienced, and practiced mindfulness in a number of different traditions. The ancient Zen Buddhism tradition, along with the more current work of Jon Kabat Zinn and his Mindfulness Based Stress Reduction (MBSR) program, have become very popular approaches to the practice of mindfulness. Although these practices have become an accepted entryway into mindfulness practice, my experience of this powerful practice was awakened by a different source.

My background in mindfulness training originally began through the study of and initiation into the ancient Hawaiian healing system known as Huna Kane. The practice of Huna Kane, in short, is translated into English as "the inner knowing of the higher self." It's a way of coming into alignment with all parts of ourselves and of waking up to the present moment, experiencing the mind, body, and spirit of who we are. Throughout this book, I will refer to this system of healing as I shed a new perspective on mindfulness. In addition, I will draw on my training as a mindfulness coach and yoga instructor, both of which have deep roots in my mindfulness practice and training.

It's from these origins that I bring to you a new perspective on this powerful practice of mindfulness. Through this book, I hope to clarify and demystify the word "mindfulness," which has taken on such popularity and generated buzz in many of our everyday conversations. My intention is to give you a solid, five-step framework to integrate this powerful practice into your daily life and remind you of who you already are, naturally.

As author Bryon Kate so wisely suggests, "The definition of insanity is to believe that you need something you don't have." I would suggest, as you will quickly discover in the reading of this book, you already have everything you need within yourself in this present moment. Now is the moment of true power. Are you ready to step fully into it and be free of this current rush to an imaginary finish line?

CHAPTER 1

THE FOUNDATION OF MINDFULNESS

*Learn how to see. Realize that
everything is connected to everything else.*
—Leonardo da Vinci

I was failing French class in seventh grade. Unfortunately, studying French did not come easily to me, and halfway through the year I realized I would have to pull my socks up or be doomed to repeat the entire academic year. Because I feared failing French class, I approached my teacher and asked if I could do an extra assignment to get my overall grade up. Without hesitation, my teacher agreed and told me I could submit an extra, creative project in French. Off I went to figure out what on earth I would do to get my grade up.

During the quest to figure out my extra credit project, I discovered my mother's old Yamaha guitar, which had been collecting dust for years in our attic. One evening, while practicing the three or four chords I had learned, it dawned on me that I could make music a part of my extra credit assignment. Without second guessing my idea, I asked my mother to help me translate Bob Dylan's song "Blowing in the Wind" into French.

I recorded the song on a cassette tape and handed it in. To my surprise, I was given an A+ on the assignment, which brought my overall mark up to a D-. I was so pleased with myself; I would be able to pass the academic year and carry on to eighth grade. What resulted next was a pivotal moment in my life that would forever change me and introduce me to the foundations of mindfulness.

Upon grading my project, my teacher asked if I wanted to perform the song live, in front of the entire student body at the next school assembly. I am not sure what came over me to say yes, but the next thing I knew I was standing at the front of the school gymnasium, watching students flood into the gym for assembly. As I watched this sea of faces, I could feel my heart rate increase; my hands started shaking, my breath was shallow, and I became very nervous. Most noticeably, a loud internal voice that only I could hear screamed at me to run for the hills!

Following a brief introduction by the school principal, I walked out and felt all eyes upon me. I performed my version of "Blowing in the Wind," which translated into "Soufflée Dans Le Vent," and before the first verse was complete, my worst nightmare came true. I could hear snickering as restlessness set in among the students. It was clear that this was not going over very well, and the voice in my head got even louder, insisting I soon would be the laughing stock of the entire school.

As chaos erupted in the gym, I battled my way through the song, but then I heard another intuitive whisper, much like the gentle whisper I had heard when I first decided to take on this project. This unseen whispering voice gently nudged me to begin playing a different song, "The Cat Came Back" by well-known children's entertainer Fred Penner.

In a last-minute attempt to gain back the ears and respect of the restless students, I broke into the song my intuition suggested.

To my surprise, within a few moments the energy in the gymnasium shifted. It was as if magic came over the room. Not only did I gain back their attention, but the entire student body started singing along with me. I remember, in that moment, looking out at all the students singing along and thinking to myself, "*This* is what I want to do for the rest of my life!"

Something magical and powerful happens when a good song comes on and everyone starts singing along. It's almost as if all the things that separate us on the surface—whether race, gender, political preference, or religious beliefs—fade away, and for the short period of time we all sing along, we realize we are connected to something much deeper than the surface level most of us operate from. We may even sense something unconsciously orchestrating our day-to-day lives that somehow perfectly aligns all the pieces of our life together. So often, we are too busy to recognize this connected energy, which is also responsible for the rising and setting of the sun, the blooming of every flower, and the breath we all share. Yet, it's out of awareness and connection to this unseen presence in each of us that a mindfulness practice awakens.

This theme of connection has led me to discover the principles of mindfulness I intend to share with you. I hope to remind you of who you were created to be and inspire you to live a life of pure magic and possibility. Through understanding and remembering our connection to everything around us, we can engage with intentional living and find fulfillment, both within and around us. Awareness of our inherent connection is the foundation of mindfulness and the beginning of waking up to who we really are, thus living an inspired life.

CHAPTER 2

IKA PONO MEA

*Accept what is, let go of what was,
and have faith in what will be.*
—Sonia Ricotti

A few other significant moments of connection in my life have led me to discover what it means to live mindfully. For the past twenty years, I have performed as a professional musician in the band Keith and Renee (formally known as Easily Amused). I met Renee in 1996 at a small church in Ile Des Chenes, Manitoba. From this initial meeting, we decided to form a band and eventually went on to record and release six complete full-length albums, traveling to many parts of the world, performing music together.

During our travels, we experienced a synchronicity I attribute to the vulnerable act of putting ourselves in rental cars and airplanes to explore the world as artists. During our travels, it always seemed like the right people would show up exactly when they were needed. Events and opportunities would present themselves in an almost magical way that could not have been pre-calculated or simply the result of being world travelers. I remember our tour van being stolen along with all our musical equipment in a hotel parking lot near Philadelphia. But in less than twenty-four hours, complete strangers provided us with accommodations and assistance to get home. Within the span of a few months, most of our equipment was found and shipped back to us, along with the stolen van.

On another occasion, we had the opportunity to share the stage with one of my musical mentors and Canadian songstress, Jann Arden. Not only did Renee and I get to tour with Jann across western Canada, but we got to sing with her on the duet "Unloved," which she originally recorded with 70's star Jackson Browne.

Through my travels with the band, I came to discover that the world is one degree of separation. Ultimately, we're all connected by an intangible source that is moving the pieces around. Performing around the world with Renee, it seems the ideal characters always presented themselves to assist me in learning life's most important lessons.

My Huna Kane teacher often uses the Hawaiian phrase "Ika pono mea," which translates as, "Everything is working out perfectly on time." As I look back on my life and significant events, I can now see it all happened in the spirit of ika pono mea, with no accidents. Everything truly happened in perfect timing to lead me to this place of practicing and living the mindfulness lifestyle.

It is no coincidence that you picked up this book and are now awakening to this new practice of mindfulness. The words you are reading and the place in which you find yourself are exactly what is supposed to be. It's my hope that you will become more and more aware that life has no ordinary moments. You live an extraordinary life—if you are paying attention.

CHAPTER 3

MY *Canadian Idol* FAMILY

Always believe that something wonderful is about to happen.
—**Sukhraj Dhillon**

B ack in 2006, I spent a summer singing and competing on the reality television show *Canadian Idol*. I decided to audition for the show because I was turning twenty-eight, and apparently after twenty-eight you're no longer considered a rock star. To my surprise, I passed the first few auditions and found myself on a plane, flying from Winnipeg to Toronto to compete with the final top twenty-two contestants on the program. This meant I would be singing a solo song every week on live television in front of two million Canadians. Little did I know at the time, but two of my greatest learnings about mindfulness came out of this experience.

The first learning came to me after spending time with renowned vocal coach Debra Byrd. Debra has coached some of the greatest singers on the planet and I was fortunate enough to work with her during my time on *Canadian Idol*. Each week, I was given fifteen minutes with Debra to run through my featured performance and receive her feedback. During our first session together, I arrived at the rehearsal with a very busy mind. There were four television cameras filming me along with a whole group of other crew members observing my every move. Among all the chaos, I began to sing my selected song of the week for Debra. Within the first few lines of the song, Debra interrupted me and exclaimed, "Stop!" I immediately stopped singing even though my mind continued to race. Debra took both of my hands and asked me to breathe a deep breath with her. We took three deep breaths together and as we did, all my anxiety faded away and I felt myself become very present. Following our third breath together, Debra looked deeply into my eyes and gently whispered the following words to me, "Now sing." I immediately felt a peacefulness come over me. As I began to sing the song, I could tell that something had shifted within me. I felt more present to the music I was singing and felt deeply connected to the words in a way that I hadn't before. The music came alive within me, and I felt the power that comes with showing up fully present in the moment.

The second mindful learning from my *Canadian Idol* experience took place when I first arrived at the studio in Toronto. I was given free tickets to give to friends and family who might want to come and watch the live taping. At the time, I barely knew anyone in Toronto, as most of my friends and family lived back in my hometown of Winnipeg. Upon receiving the free tickets, I also received an inner, intuitive whisper that suggested I go out on the streets of Toronto and hand out the tickets to random strangers.

I decided to act on this intuition and handed out the tickets to several people on the streets of Toronto. The next day, following the live taping of the show, I watched the rerun of my performance. As I was singing my solo, the camera panned over to the group of random strangers in the audience whom I had given tickets to. The caption on the television read, "Keith's friends and family." Although these strangers were not immediate family members, or even friends for that matter, this memory is a reminder that we are all connected. We are all family. This, once again, is the foundational awareness that leads to a mindfulness practice.

CHAPTER 4

CONNECTED IN KENYA

Relationships are all there is. Everything in the universe only exists because it is in relationship to everything else. Nothing exists in isolation. We have to stop pretending we are individuals that can go it alone.

—Margaret J. Wheatley

One final story reminds me of how connected we all are. It began in 2008, when Renee and I received a phone call from a young man named Craig Kielburger.

At the age of twelve, Craig became aware of child labor practices after reading an article in *The Toronto Star* about a boy from Pakistan. The boy, also twelve, had been murdered for speaking out about child labor. Upon learning about this tragic event, Craig gathered fellow classmates and started a group called Free the Children. The group was formed to raise awareness of and find solutions to child labor issues.

What started as a small group at his school has, over time, expanded to reach and assist over one million people around the world. Thanks to their various initiatives, Free the Children has provided education to children in developing countries and empowered the impoverished with clean water sources and health supplies. What started in the imagination of one twelve-year-old boy has expanded to become the largest network of children helping children through education.

Craig reached out to Renee and me, expressing how much he enjoyed our music, and invited us to take part in a volunteer work trip with Free the Children to Kenya. What started as a three-week volunteer trip resulted in two full summers of volunteer work in the Masai Mara region of Kenya. Being in Kenya was a life-changing experience for me. Every day, Renee and I worked together with a group of volunteers in the local community to build schools for the children there. On the weekends, we visited the local market where the community gathered to shop for basic necessities.

My first visit to the market was an eye-opening experience. I had never seen this degree of poverty firsthand. I wandered the streets of the market and witnessed people selling used clothing and food that was rotting, all in an effort to make a bit of income to survive another day. Although we were surrounded by poverty and extremely harsh living conditions, what struck me most was that despite all the poverty, the local people seemed to have an inherent joy within them. The local people in the market would gather, sing songs, and dance together, with a deep feeling of community and connection filling the air.

The energy from the local people inspired me so much that I found myself dreaming about how amazing it would be for Renee and me to bring our guitars into the market and play music with the locals. The following weekend, we decided to make this dream a reality and brought our guitars to the marketplace.

What continued in the market that day was a beautiful exchange of music and dance. The locals taught us songs, and we also shared music with them. Although we didn't speak the same language, we connected through the power of song, dance, and laughter. It was a magical exchange.

Immediately after the jam session in the market, a man who was also volunteering with Free the Children approached Renee and me. He explained that he had come to volunteer for a few weeks on behalf of a company he owned back in his hometown of Dubai. He proceeded to ask us if we would be interested in flying to Dubai, with all expenses paid, to perform our music for the staff of his company at an upcoming event he was organizing. The next thing we knew, Renee and I were on a five-hour plane ride to Dubai.

Upon arrival, we stepped off the plane and were immediately greeted by giant skyscrapers, brand-new cars, and "all you can eat" buffets, with some of the freshest food I had ever seen. Beyond this, there was even an artificial ski slope built inside a local shopping mall, which felt more like a king's palace. After spending two months in Kenya, it was culture shock to arrive in a city with such extreme wealth.

Despite the imbalance of wealth between Kenya and Dubai, both places confirmed for me the principle and foundation of mindfulness, which states that we are all connected. Renee and I played the same songs in Dubai as we did in Kenya, and we had the same reaction from the people. We watched people smiling, dancing, and singing along with our music. In those moments, while the music was playing, it didn't matter whether one was rich or poor, male or female, of a different culture or race, or of a different skin color. The music was somehow able to transcend all the surface traits that normally separate us.

Upon witnessing and participating in these experiences, I was forever changed. I came to see that we all are inextricably connected by an invisible source that I have come to call oneness.

CHAPTER 5

THE FIVE-STEP MAKING SENSE OF MINDFULNESS FRAMEWORK

All is connected. No one thing can change by itself.
—Paul Hawken

Being "mindful" can mean something different to everyone, as there are many interpretations of this word. Full courses have been developed around this practice, and many different cultures in our world have based their practices and beliefs around this one word. Through my experiences, I have come to develop a new, personal practice and understanding of the word "mindfulness."

In the remaining pages, I will present to you a concrete, five-step framework to make sense of "mindfulness." I have found from firsthand experience that applying these five principles to your everyday life will transform you and serve as a foundation, empowering you to navigate every experience that comes your way.

CHAPTER 6

WHAT'S YOUR DREAM?

What if you slept, and what if in your sleep you dreamed and what if in your dream you went to Heaven, and there plucked a strange and beautiful flower, and what if when you awoke you had that flower in your hand, ah, what then?
—**Samuel Taylor Coleridge**

Principle 1: Everything Begins as an Inner Dream

What if I asked you, "What's your dream?" What would your immediate response be? In almost every presentation and workshop I give, this is one of the first questions I ask the audience. Over the years, I have been blown away by what happens when I ask this question. It opens people up and deepens the conversation almost instantly. Pondering our personal dreams moves things to a deeper level, as it makes one look at the heart of the matter: What is it I truly want?

It has been suggested that everything around us is alive, aware, and dreaming. As you gaze around the physical space you are in right now, consider that everything you are looking at originated first in someone's imagination. The chair you are sitting on was once a dream in someone's imagination. Before this, the inventor was probably tired of sitting on the ground or standing on his feet. He went inward, to his imaginative dream place, and created the idea of four legs and a seat, thinking, "A place to sit would be a great invention!" From the book you are currently reading to the pen used to record these words, it all originated from an inner place I will refer to as "dream time."

Consider the word "imagination." When broken down, this powerful word splits off into two very powerful words. Can you guess the two words? Imagination is made up of the words "image" and "in." Anytime we go *inside* our minds and mentally see *images* (good or bad), we begin the process of dreaming. The images we place in our mind will form our future inner dreams.

The home you're living in, the food that you eat, the clothes you're wearing, and the car you drive were once only ideas in someone's mind. Even the very essence of who you are—your skin, your bones, your face, and the hair on your head—at one point did not exist. Yet, somehow, two people got together (I will spare you the details) and dreamed the birth of you into being.

The poet William Blake powerfully writes, "That which is now proven was only once imagined." To dream is our essence. We are dreamers who are constantly creating and dreaming our thoughts into reality. Even in this moment, if your mind has started wandering off into a daydream of some sort, you are creating and dreaming from an inner place of imagination. The world around us was all created by dreams and imagination—two words, which, to me, are unanimous.

After years of asking the "what's your dream" question in my workshops, I have heard diverse answers with many different interpretations. One person will respond with a desire to travel to Europe, while another will express her desire to watch her children grow up to be healthy and happy. Someone else may speak to the dream of wanting to have a good night's sleep and no longer feel burned out and exhausted in life.

As I personally reflect on this question, some of my current dreams include opening a yoga studio and retreat center on Kaanapali Beach in Maui, Hawaii, hosting a PBS and Netflix special on mindfulness, jamming out to a few Beatles songs with Paul McCartney, and finishing the writing of this book.

Mindfulness Challenge

As you reflect on how everything begins as a dream, I invite you to consider what you're currently dreaming about. Write down at least twenty possible responses to the question, "What is your dream?" Don't limit or second guess yourself, but simply write your initial gut responses and see what you discover. With no right or wrong answer, every thought is a possibility.

We are dreamers by our very nature. The entire universe is dreaming. In the ancient Hawaiian culture, people believed that the beginning of day was marked by the sunset at night. This is completely opposite of what we have come to know as the beginning of the day, marked by a morning sunrise in North American culture. According to Serge Kahili King, "For the poetic Hawaiians of old, nighttime became a symbol of the inner world." As the sun went down below the horizon in ancient Hawaii, this marked the beginning of a new day.

Symbolically and literally, as the sun goes down in the evening, we enter a place of inner dream time and can create new possibilities in our imagination. Whether it's a random, fleeting thought, a daydream, or a night dream, everything does begin as an inner dream. Like a spark from no-thing, our imagination is triggered and ideas form, becoming the foundation and primary seedlings for what we will see manifested in our lives.

Our imaginations are powerful instruments, capable of creating anything we truly want to experience in this reality. Thus, in a mindfulness practice, it becomes essential to monitor our inner dreams and make sure they are in alignment with the way we want our lives to unfold.

According to the ancient Hawaiians, as the sun comes up over the horizon, it's the afternoon of the day. The sunrise both symbolically and literally represents our inner dreams manifesting outwardly into the external world around us. For anything to appear externally in the physical world, it must first be imagined in dream time.

During the winter months in Hawaii (December-March), if you stand at the shore of any beach and look out toward the ocean, you may see humpback whales breaching offshore. It's quite a miraculous wonder that these massive creatures can muster up the energy and power to propel themselves into the air as they express such a beautiful dance of joy. When these magnificent creatures breach above the water, we see a powerful symbol of mindfulness.

Principle 1 declares that everything begins as an inner dream. As whales swim beneath the surface of the water, they symbolize the inner thoughts in our mind, which over time become expressed and realized as they rise out of the water and manifest in the external world. Every moment of the day, our thoughts become things. But for anything to become realized in the external world, it must first be imagined within the garden of our mind.

To become a master of mindfulness practice, the concept of inner dreaming is an essential practice to apply and understand. In our culture, many of us are quite disconnected from the belief that everything around us has been created by the thoughts within our minds. In contrast to organic inspiration, one does not have to venture far to be told by society what to think, how to feel, and how to behave.

We are up against the conditioning of our culture and its pressures to conform to a specific way of being. Television commercials, advertisements, and the opinions of other people in our social circles are all external triggers that shape who we decide to become. Many times, we take on the beliefs that are spoon fed to us, without noticing that these external suggestions are shaping the thoughts in our inner dream space. In Principle 1 of mindfulness, you must learn to operate independently of the external opinion of others—unless you consciously decide you want to adopt the collective opinion.

We become what we think about. Therefore, where we choose to focus our thoughts and energy will determine, to a great extent, what will manifest in our lives. If you're willing to accept this truth, you will wake up and realize that you no longer have to adopt the opinions of others or the cultural conditioning placed upon you. Instead, you can mindfully choose what you want to dream about regularly. You are the dreamer! You create your reality! The thoughts you choose to think will form your experience of reality. Therefore, as an inner dreamer, you must wake up and dream with intent. Otherwise, you will dream on behalf of the external world's desires and demands, which may not align with the inner calling whispering inside your own soul.

Signs of a Mindful Inner Dreamer

Someone mindfully practicing the principle of inner dreaming will likely experience the following conditions on a regular basis:

1. **A merging of inner thoughts and external reality.** Mindful inner dreamers know their thoughts and words are consistently shaping the type of world they will experience on a day-to-day basis. As a result, they regularly find themselves seeing and

experiencing in the outer world—almost instantaneously—what they have been dreaming about in their minds.

2. **A decreased need for approval.** Mindful inner dreamers know that approval from others is of little importance compared to what is deep within their soul, longing to be expressed. Instead of conforming to the pressures of the external world, inner dreamers beat to the rhythm of their own inner drum.

3. **A strong belief in no limits.** The thoughts mindful inner dreamers think and the feelings they feel are energizing and make them come alive. They know that what they truly want is already on its way and everything is possible.

4. **A freedom from doubt.** Mindful inner dreamers do not doubt their ability to intentionally create and manifest. They unwaveringly believe that their thinking can create the world in which they wish to live.

5. **A flow of creative genius.** Inner dreamers find themselves regularly answering the question, "What do I want to create?" The answer is then dreamed into being.

6. **A feeling of being "already here."** Mindful inner dreamers assume their wishes are already fulfilled. Even if the dream has yet to appear in the outer world, they expect the best possible outcomes to appear at the perfect time, and they act as if what they want is already on its way or has arrived.

7. **A deep experience of faith.** Mindful inner dreamers act on pure inner faith and believe in their ability to create their reality. They are confident and trust themselves to live the life they have been imagining. They believe the acronym for FAITH stands for Finding Answers In The Heart.

8. **An assurance that comes from robust self-esteem.** These beings have mastered the art of believing in themselves at all costs. Even when no one else understands or supports their

vision, these dreamers stay true to inner confidence and remain steady in their self-esteem. They are relentless in the pursuit of realizing their inner visions.

9. **A conviction that miracles happen.** A mindful inner dreamer experiences miracles on a regular basis. They attract amazing opportunities in a manner that can almost appear as magic to the outside world. Inner dreamers make what seems impossible come true.

10. **An awareness of symbols and confirmations.** Mindful inner dreamers are regularly given symbols and signs by the outside world to affirm and support what they have been dreaming about. These symbols and confirmations will come in many different forms and will resonate deeply with the inner dreamer, on a level only they can understand and interpret.

CHAPTER 7

A BIRTH STORY:
A MIRACLE MANIFESTED

Never give up. Great things take time.
—**Dhiren Prajapati**

A few years ago, I was coaching a client who came to me with a major dilemma. To protect her privacy, I will call this client Sarah. From an early age, Sarah had a dream of being a mother and raising a child. As she sat in my office, she described to me every detail of what she imagined her child would one day look like. She said that for as long as she could remember, she had a recurring dream of a baby boy with bright red hair and big blue eyes. This image appeared so vividly and regularly in Sarah's mind, even as a young child, that she knew she was destined to be a mother one day.

Sarah arrived in my office at the age of twenty-eight. Much to her disappointment, she had never truly experienced a menstrual cycle, and her desire to have a child seemed next to impossible. She had come to seek emotional support after this upsetting truth was confirmed by her doctor, who said she would be unable to conceive.

As Sarah shared her situation with me, I could feel her deep heartache over this conflict. She had an inner knowing that she was destined to give birth to a beautiful child, yet all the signs and conditions needed to birth this dream into a reality were deemed impossible.

As I got to know Sarah over the next few coaching sessions, she shared a bit more about her life, which was extremely stressful with a demanding job as a film producer. Her job required long hours and created pressure as she rushed to meet numerous deadlines and expectations. Her diet was imbalanced, and she often lost sleep as she worked late into the night, neglecting to take breaks or relax.

As we continued to discuss her current life situation, it became clear to both of us that she was living the life of a workaholic. She was filling all her time and space with busy work and checking items off her to-do lists. Through some powerful questions, Sarah came to see that these workaholic patterns originated from an unconscious decision she had made for herself. To avoid the lingering pain and embarrassment from her inability to menstruate and become a mother, Sarah had unconsciously decided that she would work away her pain and find her worth in her job.

Unfortunately, this lifestyle caused much stress and burnout, which ultimately left Sarah even more unhappy, sitting in my office with a major dilemma. Sarah felt cheated and isolated from all the other women in her life because she was not experiencing the "normal" course of events. As a result, she built up her sense of worth by performing her job at a very high level, becoming one of the best in her field.

Over our time working together, we decided to focus on Sarah's workaholic patterns and see if we could untangle the knots tying her up inside. We worked on creating more space in her life, space she was so desperately seeking. I challenged her to turn off her phone regularly, work fewer hours, take breaks, schedule relaxation time, and establish better eating habits.

Before long, Sarah shifted. The woman who had sat in my office with a frantic, high-strung demeanor was transformed into a relaxed, almost Zen-like woman. One of the most transformative challenges I gave to Sarah was to spend time listening to her physical body and its intuitive wisdom. In the session following this challenge, Sarah returned to my office with a major breakthrough, an "aha" moment.

Through listening to her body's intuitive wisdom, Sarah experienced a major insight. By slowing down and listening to her body's intuition, Sarah heard a message that came as a silent whisper from within her. The whisper told her that the reason she had not experienced her menstrual cycle was because she had never truly given her body a chance to be heard, loved, and respected.

Shortly after this session, Sarah experienced her cycle for the first time ever; it was an absolute miracle. Two years following this breakthrough, Sarah and her husband conceived, and despite all the discouragement from medical professionals, Sarah gave birth to a redheaded, blue-eyed baby boy.

Some may call this story a miracle, and although it definitely is, this story is also further proof that everything begins as an inner dream. Even in a situation where all odds appear to be against you, you will ultimately become what you regularly believe and dream about inwardly. To practice mindfulness Principle 1, you must be willing to defy all odds and hold the vision you are dreaming for yourself at the forefront of your imagination. What you focus on will ultimately become your reality, even if it appears to be otherwise at the moment.

Step 1 of the mindfulness framework invites you to be a conscious inner dreamer. When you choose to step into the active role of inner dreaming, you will create the life you desire and imagine for yourself. The following is an excerpt taken directly from my morning journal as

I reflected upon what took place for Sarah and her miraculous inner dream. I am certain that beneath the surface of who we appear to be, there is much more taking place that will consciously awaken within us when we embrace our inherent ability to inner dream.

Under this skin and these bones, you are unlimited potential. Timeless, effortless, fearless, and complete love. You are creative and expansive and have no limits when you recognize this essential truth. You no longer stress about fitting in or being accepted by the world around you. This is because you come to realize that you are the world. You are the energy, the force that is underneath the beating of your heart, the force that continuously grows your fingernails and hair. You are the force behind all melodies sung by the birds, the light streaming down from the sky. You are everything, and everything is you.

CHAPTER 8

DREAM BUSTERS

Nothing in life is to be feared, it is only to be understood. Now is the time to understand more, so that we may fear less.
—Marie Curie

N ow that you have come to know that everything begins as an inner dream before it manifests in the outer world, you have an important question to consider: "What gets in your way of getting what you truly want in your life?" I would like you to take a few moments and make a laundry list of some of the things that get in your way (besides the laundry). Once you have made your list of dream busters, read on and notice commonalities between your responses and the top responses from the people I interviewed.

After interviewing clients and friends, I compiled a list of common road blocks that prevent us from manifesting our inner dreams. Let's take a look.

Ultimate Dream Busters:

1. **Time.** Have you ever felt you lack the time to do everything you want? Do you find yourself dreaming about possibilities, only to shelve the ideas, convinced you don't have enough time? Do you commonly find yourself thinking, "I will enjoy myself and be fulfilled as soon as I finish my current task"? Do you also find that you never really arrive where you want to be or get around to what you truly want to do because of time? If you're experiencing a poverty of time in your life, you are not alone. This is a very common dream buster for many people.

2. **Money.** Lack of money and resources is another top dream buster. I have struggled with this one in my own life. As I mentioned earlier, one of my current dreams is to open a wellness retreat center in Maui. I imagine a center where like-minded people can come together to explore various wellness programs with top facilitators from around the world. I also imagine this center playing host to a world-class yoga studio and a hotel to accommodate guests while they visit the center. I often catch myself dreaming about this vision, only to quickly knock it down, focusing instead on the large sum of money needed to fulfill such a lofty undertaking. Many of us find ourselves in this common pattern: We get a powerful idea but quickly dismiss it, fearing a lack of money.

3. **The opinion of others.** Many of us grew up believing that the good opinion of others was more important than our own opinion. Whether it was our parents, our siblings, our teachers, or friends, many learn from a young age to put others' opinions ahead of their own. Many of us have lived our lives based on how we think other people want us to be.

   Consider how many people have denied expressing their natural gifts, talents, and ideas to the world because of fear of what others might think. Many have suffocated inner dreams by living a life dominated by the fear of being judged and deemed unworthy.

This particular dream buster reminds me of the Harry Chapin song "Mr. Tanner." The song is about a man who ran a dry-cleaning shop in Midwest America and would sing while pressing the customers' clothes. Over time, the locals in his hometown became aware of his talent and convinced him to sing at a concert in New York. He follows through with their suggestion to perform a concert in New York and comes back to his hometown defeated by the critics who gave him a bad review. The song concludes saying that Mr. Tanner never sang again, apart from late at night when his shop was dark and closed.

This song exemplifies what happens when we let the criticism and opinions of others override our inner dreams. Consider how many Einstein-like minds are simply silenced because of the dream-busting fear that they will be criticized by other people. How many composers, authors, bands, inspirational speakers, and so on are voiceless because they would rather remain silent than face the opinions and judgment of their peers?

Millions of untold stories, unrecorded albums, unwritten songs and poems, undiscovered scientific breakthroughs, and unrealized dreams have withered away because of this particular dream buster. I read an anonymous quote just this morning on the tag of my tea bag: "Be who you want to be, not who they choose to see." How timely!

4.   **Fear.** The acronym for fear in the mindfulness framework stands for False Evidence Appearing Real. Michel de Montaigne, a philosopher of the French Renaissance said, "My life has been filled with terrible misfortune; most of which never happened."

Researchers at Cornell University studied people over an extended period of time and found that 85 percent of what subjects worried about never happened. Moreover, the study found that 79 percent of the subjects handled the 15 percent that did happen better than they thought they could. I often think about how much energy gets wasted worrying about things that never end up happening the way we feared they might.

Just last week, I found myself in a pattern of worry when I realized that I had accidentally double booked two coaching clients in my schedule at the same time. Upon realizing this double booking, I worried all night about the worst-case scenarios that might result the next morning. It was too late at night to call either client and tell him about the scheduling mishap. Telling them the next morning would also be unprofessional, as it would be very short notice. There I was, restless in my bed, worrying about how I would deal with this situation. I was convinced that I would lose one or both clients because of this mistake.

The next morning arrived, and to my surprise, I received a phone call from one of the clients I had double booked, explaining that he had come down with the flu and needed to reschedule the appointment. In that moment, after the instant feeling of relief, it dawned on me that I had wasted a whole night of my life, along with a lot of energy, worrying about a scenario that simply did not happen the way I feared it would.

Consider that when we are completely present in the mind and body, it's impossible to experience fear because fear can only operate when we are replaying an event from the past or worrying about a future moment. Fear simply can't exist when we are fully present in the moment. Fear is frequently to blame for busting apart our dreams and corroding our hopes with worst-case scenarios.

CHAPTER 9

THE ULTIMATE DREAM BUSTER

Fear defeats more people than any other one thing in the world.
—**Ralph Waldo Emerson**

We see that time, money, the opinions of others, and fear are among some of the top barriers that can hinder us from pursuing our dreams. Through the writings of Swiss psychiatrist Carl Jung, I have discovered a special name that encapsulates all the dream busters that get in my way and stop me from getting what I want out of life. I have come to know this ultimate dream buster as the "Saboteur." You can imagine this force as a character, an antagonist who opposes you at every turn. Other names of this adversary include: "the Inner Critic," "the Ego," "the Gremlin," and "the Shadow Self." Whatever name you choose for the self-doubt and worry that plagues you, the presence of this ultimate dream buster is important to recognize because we all have a form of it playing out in our lives.

The Saboteur lives in our consciousness and makes us second guess our every thought and desire in life. Some people experience this character as a loud voice that chatters away in their head, while others may experience the Saboteur as a feeling or sensation in their body. Feelings of dread, anxiety, sadness, panic, worry, doubt, depression, hopelessness, and fear are all common signs that the Saboteur is lurking near.

For many people, the idea of an invisible character, a saboteur, in their consciousness is a very foreign concept. In fact, some are completely oblivious to the role this limiting force plays in their lives as it manipulates their dreams and desires. For those who deny altogether that they have a saboteur, I would argue that their saboteur is so engrained that it's completely intertwined with their identity.

I recently met a woman at one of my workshops who claimed she did not have a saboteur. She said she used to have a version of the Saboteur playing out in her awareness, but she dealt with it and it was no longer there. During the workshop, this woman's saboteur became very obvious to the group as she played the role of a know-it-all expert. The version of saboteur playing out in her consciousness had her believing she was better than everyone else. Although on the surface this woman appeared to have life entirely figured out, as the workshop progressed, it became obvious that her know-it-all position was actually a protective false front she put on to avoid anyone seeing her as flawed.

Little did this woman realize that her saboteur was keeping her in a state of separation, ultimately preventing her from connecting with the rest of the group in a deep and meaningful way. So many of us go through life fearful to show our true colors. Our saboteur has us believing that who we truly are is not enough—that we are unworthy, unlovable, and flawed in one way or another.

As you open your mind to the possibility that this ultimate dream buster could, in fact, be an entity in your consciousness, you may not only start seeing it in yourself, but also in the world around you. For example, do you know people who constantly share the breaking news stories and warn everyone about what a dangerous world we live in? Have you ever met someone who is continually critical of others, along with herself, and never seems to be satisfied? Gossip, separation, drama, worry, fear, and anxiety are all attributes of the Saboteur.

Saboteurs have the ability to completely silence us and convince us that all we have been dreaming about is likely not to happen. Saboteurs list all the reasons why our dreams will never become reality. Saboteurs wreak havoc with our self-esteem and convince us that we are better off to "play it safe." Saboteurs warn us that we will fail, so we might as well give up or not try at all. They know which buttons to press, so to speak, to paralyze us from taking action and stepping fully into the life we want to live. Saboteurs keep us in a false sense of safety. They convince us that if we take a risk outside of the status quo, we will somehow be in danger.

Ultimately, the Saboteur is an active character in our consciousness that represents all the dream-busting, false-evidence-appearing-real (FEAR) aspects of our lives. It's the voice or feeling that comes over you, suggesting there will not be enough time in the day to get it all done or enough money in the bank. It mocks you, saying you must try harder or be more or get more or do more. It tells you certain people don't like you or that you did a poor job at the task you were performing. It convinces you that things are going to go wrong and that much of your past could have gone differently, better. It's the voice that keeps you up at night, worrying about all the past and future problems that might arise in your life. The Saboteur can take many angles, but perhaps you are getting a glimpse into some of its common patterns. Does any of this sound familiar?

CHAPTER 10

EXPOSE THE SABOTEUR

I'm not afraid of storms, for I'm learning how to sail my ship.
—**Louisa May Alcott**

P rinciple 2 in the Making Sense of Mindfulness framework is what I refer to as "Expose the Saboteur." This principle invites us to take a hard look at the limits we have placed on ourselves and decide if we want to keep living under these conditions or stand in our full power, free of limitations and excuses. It has been suggested that when you get vulnerably close to what you want, the Saboteur gets louder, more present, and extremely persuasive. There may be certain saboteur patterns operating in your life that are so disguised, you may have come to accept them as "just the way it is."

Principle 2: Expose the Saboteur

To practice exposing the Saboteur, you must become present in the moment and pay close attention to what you are thinking and how you are feeling. I would like to offer you a few saboteur symptoms to watch out for.

Signs and Indicators That the Saboteur Is Lurking Near:

1. **Nervous laughter.** As you get close to uncomfortable edges in your life, you may find yourself laughing nervously and covering up feelings of awkwardness with levity. The Saboteur often avoids awkward scenarios by moving you to uncomfortable laughter to cover up the awkwardness.

2. **Shortness of breath.** When we get close to an edge, the Saboteur takes control and sometimes our breath shortens or even disappears. For example, many of us find that our breath becomes shallow just before we have to speak in public. The Saboteur moves us into survival mode by manipulating our natural breathing rhythm. Shortness of breath often is a strong indicator that we are right up against our fear.

3. **Busy-mind distractions.** Overthinking, excuses, and scattered thoughts are definite signs of the Saboteur's manipulative power. Thoughts of worry and panic about the past or future also indicate that a saboteur is controlling you in the present moment.

4. **Frustration and low energy.** At times, you may feel agitated, annoyed, and frustrated when a saboteur is manipulating your consciousness. You may also experience low energy levels without an explanation. Be on the lookout for a saboteur in full operation.

5. **Heart rate.** An increased heart rate is a sure sign you are going up against something that scares you. The Saboteur may be lurking when you notice your heart rate speed up.

6. **Tense muscles.** Like an increased heart rate, another physical symptom that indicates the Saboteur is near is the tightening

of muscles. Areas including the chest, shoulders, abdomen, and stomach may tighten up when a saboteur is in operation.

7. **Talking fast.** When we are nervous and uncomfortable, the Saboteur will manipulate the pace at which we speak, making us speak more quickly than normal. We may also put extra words into our sentences when being manipulated by our saboteur.

8. **Filling up time.** Saboteurs are notorious for filling our time with busy work projects. Busyness for the sake of staying busy and filling all the possible gaps with noise can be a symptom of the Saboteur.

9. **Procrastination.** Procrastination is a sure sign that the Saboteur is using avoidance and resistance to distract your consciousness. The Saboteur can convince us that we ought to delay anything that might move us closer to our true life's purpose.

10. **Butterflies.** A sign that you're crossing the line into uncomfortable territory and triggering the Saboteur is when you feel butterflies in your stomach.

11. **External approval.** When we get close to an uncomfortable edge, many of us look outside of ourselves for external validation and approval. Instead of trusting our inner intuition, we allow the Saboteur to convince us that the only way to move forward is through the approval of others. This symptom of the Saboteur can play out in many unique forms, including the wearing of a false front, which changes the way we look and ultimately gives our power away.

12. **Nervous system symptoms.** When the Saboteur is in full operation, our nervous system is often activated into fight mode. We may find ourselves involuntarily shaking, sweating, and tightening up.

Mindfulness Challenge

These are just a few of the common symptoms that can occur when the Saboteur is present in your life. What other behaviors or symptoms indicate the Saboteur is present for you? Take a few minutes and create your own list of symptoms to assist you in exposing your saboteur. In so doing, you will become mindfully aware of when you're letting false evidence appearing real (FEAR) prevent you from achieving what you truly desire.

CHAPTER 11

THE ORIGIN OF SABOTEURS

Fears are educated into us, and can, if we wish, be educated out.
—Karl Augustus

W hy do we have saboteurs in our life and where did they come from? Beyond keeping us in a false sense of safety and maintaining the status quo, the Saboteur operates according to a conditioned pattern we have learned over time and accepted as truth. Sometimes saboteur patterns form when we take a risk in our lives and fail. When we try something with all our heart and soul, but fail, we often decide that we best not try again. We simply give up. Through this decision, the Saboteur assures us that, going forward, we will remain safe and in control, but playing it safe ultimately prevents us from ever taking a risk again.

Besides our own experiences of failure, the societal beliefs of past generations are often the origins of saboteur patterns. As children, we are handed rules and regulations on what we should and shouldn't do.

The beliefs of our parents, our siblings, our peers, and the society we live in shape us to a large degree. Many times, these conditions become engrained into our DNA.

Our parents' parents—and even their parents—may have formed certain belief patterns based on experiences they had. Without consciously realizing it, past generations handed these limiting belief patterns down through the lineage to you. Although these belief patterns may have served a past generation, be careful not to adopt beliefs and rules that no longer serve you.

When I was a child, my mother told me to stay away from bees, warning me that a bee sting could really hurt me. Although a bee has never stung me, to this day, I find myself apprehensive around these beautiful creatures that magically produce honey for my toast. After years of believing a small insect—smaller than the size of my thumb— might harm me, I automatically cringe when a bee flies around me. My mother's mother most likely warned her as a child, and if I traced it back, perhaps an ancestor had a deadly reaction to a bee sting. Although the fear of a bee sting may have served an ancestor, in my own life, it prevents me from enjoying the beauty and wonder of these magnificent insects.

This example of my conditioned fear around bees is exactly how our saboteurs form. From a neurological perspective, the part of our brain that initiates our fight or flight response (known as the amygdala) can sometimes have difficulty distinguishing between a real threat and a perceived threat. Although the human brain has evolved since prehistoric times, we may occasionally find that we're still triggered into fear and fight mode without even realizing it. There's a very good chance that lions won't attack you on the street where you live, however, to the prehistoric brain, this was a real threat. In order to update our thinking patterns and shift out of fear mode, we must learn how to name our limiting beliefs and expose our saboteur.

At some point, a limiting belief was introduced to you. Taking on this limiting belief, you formed a fear through repetitive thought and/or feeling, and this limiting belief became your accepted norm, your new rule. Here are a few saboteur beliefs that Western society has adopted and likely passed on to you:

"Boys don't cry."

"Showing emotions or feelings is a sign of weakness."

"I don't have enough money."

"Life is so hard, day in and day out."

"I won't try because I'm going to fail."

"Don't give up your day job."

"The chances are slim that _____ will happen."

"That's just the way it is; it has always been this way."

"Don't embarrass yourself!"

"I'm so stupid."

"Big girls don't cry."

"Life is short, and then you die."

"No matter how hard you try, you'll never get ahead."

"I'll be stuck here forever."

"I need you to like me, or I'll fail."

Mindfulness Challenge

How did these listed beliefs become our collective truth? I invite you to spend time reflecting on the common saboteur beliefs you have adopted. See if you can trace these thoughts back to their roots. Most likely, your saboteur beliefs are no longer serving you. What are your limiting saboteur beliefs and patterns? List them now.

CHAPTER 12

JUMP OUT OF THE JAR

Avoiding danger is no safer in the long run than outright exposure.
The fearful are caught as often as the bold.
—Helen Keller

I recently came across a YouTube video published by Power Brain Education that suggested a flea can jump nearly one hundred times its height. For a human, that would be the equivalent of jumping to the top of a skyscraper. If you put a flea in a jar, it will jump right out. If you place a lid on the jar, the flea will attempt to jump out of the jar and continually hit the bottom of the lid, only to fall back down to the bottom of the jar. Over time, the flea learns that hitting the bottom of the lid is not a good idea and trains itself only to jump so high as to not hit the bottom of the lid. The YouTube video went on to explain that the amazing thing is, even if you take the lid off the jar, the flea won't jump out. It has been conditioned only to jump so high.

And so it is for humans who have been conditioned by their limiting beliefs and saboteurs to jump only so high. Our belief systems shape our reality. If you have a limiting belief cutting you off from the unlimited potential that exists outside of your jar, it will take serious, intentional effort to become aware that you're caught in a pattern of false evidence appearing real.

We are creatures of habit and belief. To truly grow and live the life we imagine for ourselves, we must be willing to expose the Saboteur. We must be courageous enough to take the lid off our jar and jump beyond where we have conditioned ourselves to stay. Are you willing to reject any limit on what is possible? Can you trust that the only limitations preventing you from living a life on purpose is your own limiting thoughts and beliefs, triggered by the Saboteur?

CHAPTER 13

CROSS THE LINE

If one advances confidently in the direction of their dreams and endeavors to live the life which they have imagined, they will be met with a success unexpected in common hours.
—**Ralph Waldo Emerson**

"I just can't do it!" she said. "I won't have enough money, and this is just way too scary to step into." Jenny's saboteur was sitting with her in my coaching office, listing all the reasons why she would be unable to expand her business and lease a new office space. "If I spend three thousand dollars a month, I won't have enough money left over to make ends meet."

As I sat there listening to Jenny's saboteur ramble on about all the scary reasons why she might fail, we both knew it was only a matter of time before she was going to press the send button on her phone and answer yes to leasing her new office space. For a full month prior to this session, Jenny had come to see me weekly and explained that her next move in business was to grow her office space. She told me that when she expanded her office space, more business would flow in, and she would take things to the next level of operation. Although she saw the ultimate potential in expanding her business space, fulfilling her aspirations seemed light years away.

As I sat there in my office, hearing yet another excuse as to why she needed to delay her next move, I stood up and grabbed a roll of masking tape from my desk. I proceeded to roll a string of tape across the floor and explained that there were two sides to the current crisis. I asked Jenny to identify what side of the tape she wanted to be on. The side of the tape she was currently sitting on represented fear, apprehension, and narrow vision. The other side, which happened to be in the sunroom of my office, looked lighter, expansive, and exciting; it represented stepping into a new chapter of her life and taking the upgraded office space.

As she held her phone in her hand, I asked her to write a yes or no response to the offer from her landlord. She hesitantly typed out a message that stated she would take the new office space. I asked her not to send the message until she felt ready to step across to the other side of the tape. I also made sure she knew that the step did not have to happen right away—or at all.

Jenny took a deep breath, stood up, courageously crossed the tape line, and pressed the send button on her phone. A huge burst of emotion filled the room as we both teared up and realized that we had witnessed the exposing of the Saboteur first hand. No longer was Jenny a slave to her saboteur mindset. She was free to expand and allow her business to prosper.

The 1841 essay "Heroism" by Ralph Waldo Emerson recommends the following: "Be true to your own act, and congratulate yourself if you have done something strange and extravagant, and broken the monotony of a decorous age. It was a high counsel I once heard given to a young person, 'Always do what you are afraid to do.'" In 1997, Mary Schmich wrote an article for the *Chicago Tribune* that begins, "Inside every adult lurks a graduation speaker dying to get out." The article continues with a list of advice aimed at young students. In this list is a quote that urges, "Do one thing a day that scares you."

I recall standing on a diving board at my family's cabin at Lake of the Woods, Ontario. It was a cool spring day, and the weather was barely warm enough for lake swimming. The longer I stood on the diving board looking out at the water, the more I found myself second guessing my decision to swim. In my mind, I began listing all the reasons why I shouldn't jump in.

To confidently cross over to the other side and take that leap of faith is to discover that what seemed to be impossible is, in actuality, life's greatest offering to us. We discover that the only limits pressing upon us are the sabotaging fears that have convinced us to remain static and stale, fears that have prevented us from growing, expanding, and fully experiencing life.

I urge you to jump off the diving board and expose the Saboteur. You'll quickly discover that the life you once only imagined will quickly become your reality. Jump in! The water is warm and ready to support you in the advancement of your inner dreams.

CHAPTER 14

PRACTICE MAKES PERFECT

Life is a mirror and will reflect back to the thinker what he thinks into it.

—Ernest Holmes

I'd like to offer you a few tips to help you "jump off the diving board" and expose your limiting beliefs. Try these mindfulness practices as you begin to expose the Saboteur.

What Does Your Saboteur Look Like?

Consider your saboteur. Is it a human form or a non-human form? Is it male or female? What colors are associated with it? Does it have a voice? If so, what does its voice sound like? If it doesn't have a voice, how does it communicate with you? Does it remind you of someone you already know? Get a clear visual of what your saboteur looks like and then draw a picture of it. This exercise can shed light on who/what has been blocking you from living your dreams.

Expose Your Saboteur in the Washroom

Ironically, I've found that the best place to practice exposing my saboteur is in the washroom, while washing my hands. Next time you wash your hands, look up. Staring you right in the face is one of the best tools you have to practice exposing your saboteur. Can you guess what this might be? The mirror! Notice that the most common reaction when looking at ourselves in the mirror is resistance and criticism.

When we look at ourselves in the mirror, almost immediately, our inner saboteur points out all the imperfections: pimples, bad hair, and excessive fat. The saboteur is always the first to judge and critique all the imperfections of our physical appearance and beyond. To stand in front of a mirror daily and affirm to yourself that you are beautiful just the way you are is a tall order—especially if your saboteur tells you this practice is as cheesy as Stuart Smalley's daily affirmations skit on *Saturday Night Live*. Although it may feel awkward at first, the practice of looking at yourself in the mirror and affirming your beauty and worth will expose the Saboteur and reestablish your real power.

A mirror is ultimately the best friend you'll ever have, as it will not judge you. It allows you to simply show up the way you are. It never speaks back to you in words but gives you its full attention by being present. Becoming friends with yourself in the mirror is one of the most important practices of mindfulness.

Notice that any resistance you feel is not coming from the mirror, for the mirror is not doing anything to you. It's simply reflecting and holding non-judgmental space. The resistance you experience is an internal saboteur. The practice of mirror work in the context of mindfulness requires us to expose and put aside the resistance that comes up. When we see past the resistance and silence the Saboteur, we discover eternal beauty, love, and inner peace.

As Marianne Williamson writes:

Our deepest fear is not that we are inadequate. Our deepest fear is that we are powerful beyond measure. It is our light, not our darkness that most frightens us . . . Your playing small does not serve the world. There is nothing enlightened about shrinking so that other people won't feel insecure around you. We are all meant to shine, as children do . . . It's not just in some of us; it's in everyone. And as we let our own light shine, we unconsciously give other people permission to do the same. As we are liberated from our own fear, our presence automatically liberates others.

I encourage you to stand in front of a mirror regularly and practice exposing your saboteur by seeing past the surface and quelling any criticism that comes up. Affirm out loud to yourself, "I love you. I really, really love you." If you can speak it from your heart and feel it in your body, knowing that the only limitation is a false saboteur discouraging you, I truly believe you will be on your way to realizing what a powerful presence you are on this planet. This is truly mindfulness practice in action.

CHAPTER 15

GIVE BIRTH TO AN OPEN MIND

Nothing is impossible, the word itself says "I'm Possible."
—**Audrey Hepburn**

I n 1977, my father was diagnosed with testicular cancer. Although I was not alive at the time, I can only imagine what a trying time this must have been for a young, twenty-five-year-old man. Chemotherapy was a new form of cancer treatment at the time, and there was uncertainty as to its side effects. With the unknown question of life or death hanging over my father, my parents struggled with major life decisions. Not only was my father battling cancer, but in the process of this battle, my mother had become pregnant. Upon advice from the doctor, my mother was encouraged to proceed with an abortion. She was told that the chances of a child being born free of brain damage and other side effects from the chemotherapy treatments my father had been receiving were slim.

Despite the recommendations from the specialists, my parents decided to go forward with birthing their first child, and into the world I arrived. I was born with a full head of red hair and an overall healthy disposition. My parents went on to have two other children, and both my brothers arrived in the world healthy and full of life. I often think about what open minds both my parents had to have to proceed when all odds were against them. If they had simply accepted the doctor's advice on the matter and not opened their minds to other possibilities, I probably would not have arrived in the world, along with my two wonderful brothers.

My father still lives to tell of the miracle healing that took place for him and my mother back in their twenties. When asked about how he beat his cancer diagnosis, my father attributes much of his miraculous healing to the power of his mindset. Aside from the medical treatment he received, he attests that his positive mindset and desire to live overrode all the odds against him. He wasn't closed off to what could be. Instead, he was open and receptive to life.

Principle 3: Open Your Mind

"Have a mind that is open to everything and attached to nothing." This quote from tantric practitioner Tilopa (circa 988-1069) exhibits a way of thinking that has sustained itself through time, and is an important component in the Making Sense of Mindfulness framework. To live mindfully requires us to open our mind to all possibilities. Too often, in this fast-paced world, we find ourselves distracted and somewhat cut off from listening to what our hearts and intuition are calling us toward. We find ourselves stuck in predictable routines, which develop as a result of our habitual thinking and unconscious acceptance of these patterns. Without always realizing it, we accept things the way they are, without question, and sometimes even fear stepping outside of our comfort zone. Consequently, we miss out on growth and creative expansion.

Developing a mindfulness lifestyle requires us to open our minds and consider all the possibilities that lie before us. Over the next few chapters, I'll explore the principle of living with an open mind by sharing stories of people who have successfully implemented this mindfulness practice into their lives, and by offering further suggestions on how to begin this powerful practice.

One of my greatest mentors and influencers is a man I first came to know through listening to his audio books in my car. Dr. Wayne Dyer was arguably one of the most influential figures in the world of self-help and motivation. Wayne's teachings and ability to share internal wisdom in an accessible and meaningful way was beyond extraordinary. I was fortunate enough to study with Wayne Dyer several times in Maui, where he lived. During his lectures, Wayne would often share inspirational quotes with his audience and encouraged people to live with an open mindset.

In 2012, Wayne Dyer was diagnosed with leukemia. He openly shared with the public that he was determined to fully recover and heal himself from his cancer. He believed his healing would come as a direct result of changing his thinking and beliefs about the disease. Through opening his mind and taking a non-traditional approach to healing his body, Wayne sought out alternative forms of healing, including a psychic surgery (performed from a distance by Brazil's well-known healer John of God), a diet change, and daily affirmations to himself, including, "I am well." While many questioned and criticized this approach to healing, Wayne held steadfast to his conviction that he could heal himself through the power of an open mind and convinced himself that he was healed from his cancer diagnosis.

On August 29, 2015, Wayne Dyer left his body. It was almost impossible to believe. A man who seemed timeless and indestructible would no longer walk on this earth. As I received the news of Wayne's death, my heart sank and tears filled my eyes. This was a man who truly impacted my life. I was certain that the cause of Wayne's death was leukemia, but much to my surprise, his cause of death was ruled a heart attack. Upon closer examination, the autopsy report indicated there was not one trace of leukemia found in his body at the time of death.

Through opening his mind, Wayne proved that the next to impossible was actually possible. By eliminating all limiting beliefs and attachments surrounding his diagnosis, Wayne proved an open mind is one of our most powerful tools. When we mindfully commit to opening our mind to what is possible, all that we desire—including the healing of a terminal disease—can manifest in our lives.

Consider what might have resulted if you hadn't opened your mind at certain times in your life. If you hadn't opened your mind, you might not be reading this book right now. You might have missed out on taking the trip of a lifetime. Without an open mind, perhaps you would have missed out on meeting the partner of your dreams. I often think that if I hadn't opened my mind, I would not be writing this book, or instructing yoga classes, or successfully working as a mindfulness coach, or recording new music, or living in my beautiful home, married to my beautiful wife.

As you look around yourself, notice that everything, including your body, could not have come to fruition if not for an open mind. The mind is a truly miraculous gift we have been given to create and imagine anything into form. The practice of mindfulness requires us to open our minds and become aware of the inner whispers and intuitions present all around us. When we learn how to work with an open mind, we awaken to wonders and miracles that can only be perceived in the present moment.

In addition, inventions such as the automobile that transports us, the television that entertains us, and the phone that connects us, wouldn't exist if their inventors hadn't kept open minds. All successful scientists know that it's the curiosity of an open mind that leads to new discoveries and breakthroughs. In contrast, it's the stubborn attachment to what already is and our closed-minded thinking that destroys all new possibilities. I'm reminded of the words proclaimed by Albert Einstein while almost giving up in his quest to prove the theory of relativity. He exclaimed, "You never fail until you stop trying." Likewise, Thomas Edison only discovered the transformative power of a light bulb because he refused to accept the idea that it was impossible: "I have learned 10,000 ways it cannot be done, and, therefore, I am 10,000 times nearer the final successful experiment."

Consider this: living with an open mind that is attached to nothing can make everything possible. I have found, in my own life, that every rejection and every "no" leads me closer to the "yes" I'm ultimately seeking. Alexander Graham Bell, the inventor of the telephone, wrote, "When one door closes, another opens; but we often look so long and so regretfully upon the closed door that we do not see the one which has opened for us."

Mindfulness Challenge

Take a few moments to ponder and write down at least twenty things that have manifested in your life because you opened your mind. This may include birthing your child, landing a successful business contract, finding the partner of your dreams, creating an invention, and so on. Notice that an open mind always holds the key to unlocking your potential.

CHAPTER 16

SUSPEND YOUR DISBELIEF

What great things would you attempt
if you knew you could not fail?
—**Robert H. Schuller**

t's much too easy to live content with how things already are, regularly stifling your dreams and ambitions. The daily grind, in combination with the mental attachments we have accepted as normal, can make it next to impossible to truly see our dreams become reality. When we suspend our disbelief and cross the line into the world of the unknown, magic appears and works with us

Such was the case for a young man from Ohio named Steven. For as long as he could remember, Steven had a childhood dream of becoming a Hollywood movie producer. As a child, he would make amateur films using a primitive camera and his powerful imagination. In 1965, Steven's family moved to California, and he enrolled in film school. How Steven became one of Hollywood's top movie directors, however, is considered a miracle to this day.

On a visit to Universal Studios as a tourist, Steven took a tram ride through the backlot to get a first-hand glance at how the world's top movies were made. While on the tram ride, despite feelings of hesitation from the Saboteur, Steven snuck off the tram and hid between two sound stages until the tour ended. He then courageously ventured into the unknown territory of Universal Studio's backlot and began greeting all the people involved in the making of films there.

It has been said that the most important person he met on his first day in the backlot was the security guard at the front gate. Following this initial visit, Steven returned to the backlot daily. It wasn't too long before he became friends with the studio's vice president at the time, Sidney Sheinberg. After seeing one of Steven's short films, Sheinberg offered him a seven-year directing contract, which ultimately led to the creation of some of the world's most successful blockbuster films, including *Jaws*, *Indiana Jones*, *The Color Purple*, *E.T.*, and *Star Wars*, to name a few.

It's not a surprise to those who understand the power of an open mind that Steven Spielberg fulfilled his ambitious vision and is now the founder of his appropriately titled company DreamWorks. Opening the mind, crossing over the line, and defying all resistance and attachments will produce miraculous results. In his book *The Laws of Success*, Paramahansa Yogananda writes, "Mind is the creator of everything. You should guide it to create only good. If you cling to a certain thought with dynamic willpower, it finally assumes a tangible outward form."

CHAPTER 17

LET IT GO AND LET IT FLOW

For it is in giving that we receive.
—St. Francis of Assisi

I n his book *The Way to Love*, Anthony de Mello writes, "Think of yourself in a concert hall listening to strains of the sweetest music when you suddenly remember that you forgot to lock your car. You are anxious about the car. You can't walk out of the hall, and you cannot enjoy the music. There you have the perfect life as it is lived by most human beings." He goes on to write, "For life to those that have the ears to hear is a symphony; but very, very rare indeed is the human being who hears the music. This is because they are busy listening to the noises that their conditioning and programming have put into their heads."

The greatest deterrent that prevents us from fulfilling our dreams and living the life we imagine is our attachments. As described in Principle 2, our attachments are best characterized as that of the Saboteur. Common attachments that prevent us from living with an open mind include beliefs such as: "I am what I do," "I am what I have and possess," and "I am what other people think of me."

Attachments rooted in these three areas of belief will keep us from experiencing and expressing our authentic selves. If we live our lives based on these attachments, we will rarely enjoy the symphony of life playing out in each moment before us. Instead, we'll find ourselves preoccupied with a past or future thought that distracts us and very often convinces us that to stay safe, we need to be cautious, overprotective, and closed-minded. Attachments keep us prisoner to narrow-minded ways of thinking about life.

As mentioned earlier, money is a major attachment for many, and is at the root of most internal and external conflicts in the world. Many strong beliefs and attachments are associated with this colored paper we have collectively agreed to place value on. In my own life, I've found myself worrying about money and trying to control this invisible energy. My perspective on money has shifted significantly as I've learned to apply Principle 3: Open Your Mind.

It was a Thursday evening, and I was having dinner with a good friend, whom I hadn't seen in quite some time. We sat at the dinner table, sharing stories and catching up on each other's lives. As we conversed, my friend announced that she would soon be moving from Winnipeg to New York City to pursue her dream of becoming a professional singer/ songwriter. She explained that her dream had always been to play music professionally, and New York City kept coming to mind as the next place to truly work toward making her vision a reality.

As she spoke about her ambitious dream, my friend also listed all the doubts and reservations she had about making this significant move. Her main concern was that she would not have enough money to pay her bills in one of the most expensive cities in the world. As I listened to my friend's fears about money, a silent beckoning entered my awareness. It was a very quick intuition that floated across my mind. I had a hundred-dollar American bill stored in my wallet that was left over from my most recent trip to the United States. I had kept the bill in my wallet for quite some time and hadn't really given it much thought until this moment.

Sitting across from my friend, I felt a deep impulse within me to give her the hundred dollars as a gift and symbol of abundance. The gift would be to reassure her that she would be taken care of in the pursuit of her dreams. But almost immediately, I felt the Saboteur listing all the reasons why I shouldn't act on this impulse: "One hundred dollars is a lot of money to give away when you have expenses and debts of your own to pay!"

Despite my saboteur's inner chatter, I decided to defy all the mental noise in my mind. My intuition was just too strong to ignore this inner request. I reached into my pocket, and while my friend was in mid-sentence, I handed over the money. I assured her that she was going to be taken care of, and that this hundred-dollar bill was a symbol of prosperity and abundance in this new dream she was pursuing.

A few weeks following our dinner, I was met with quite a surprise. I found myself just south of Winnipeg in a small music venue. I'd been hired to play music at a wedding reception for a couple I had met a few years prior. About halfway through the evening, a man in the crowd came up to me and placed a hundred-dollar bill on the table beside me. He told me it was a tip for the great music I was playing. All of a sudden, I realized that this was the law of circulation in full effect. I was instantly reminded that when I let go of all I'm attached to and trust my instincts, unlimited potential lies before me.

When I truly open my mind beyond all my reservations and attachments, I'm met with a universe that reflects back with an open mind, reminding me that in the flow, all things are possible. In her book *The Magic Path of Intuition*, Florence Shinn writes, "The game of life is a game of boomerangs. Whatever you send out comes back." Remember, with a mind open to everything and attached to nothing, all things—including the flow of money—are possible.

CHAPTER 18

AN OPEN MIND IN DREAM TIME

See yourself in a blade of grass, a laughing child, a homeless soul, a thousand-year-old tree. It is all you!
—Keith Macpherson

Consider that we spend approximately one-fourth of our lives in dream time. Every evening when we close our eyes and sink into the unconscious world of sleep, our imaginations are given permission to create and run wild. In dream time, no limits exist. Have you ever considered what can take place in the span of one minute while in dream time? In one minute while dreaming, you can be in different bodies and different locations. You can explore every island of Hawaii, all parts of Europe, and visit every state across the United States. You can travel to places you have never been, places that might not even exist on this planet we call Earth.

In the span of one minute in dream time, you can fly like a bird or swim like a dolphin. You can take on the role of a rock star, performing in front of a large stadium of people. You can be the leader of any country and then change careers multiple times. You can have the best sex of your life and eat any kind of food, without ever waiting for it to be cooked. You can date or marry the ideal partner, and have all the time in the world to share together. The possibilities are endless. In dream time, anything can happen because linear time is no longer a barrier. We can be anything we want, experience anything we want, and have everything we desire—without needing to deal with the frustrations and interruptions of our real, waking life.

Beyond this, it's also important to consider how our physical body reacts when we're dreaming. Have you ever noticed that your physical body interprets your dreams as if they are actually happening in real life? While we're dreaming, the body often acts in accordance to what we're dreaming about. For example, consider a dog sleeping on the floor, fast asleep. Have you ever seen his paws moving in a quick, circular motion? It appears that the dog's body thinks it's running when, in actuality, the dog is only dreaming about running.

Have you ever witnessed someone sleeping who appears to be having a dream about flying? His arms may twitch and lift like wings. His legs may even move or kick—all because his physical body is convinced that he is actually flying. The body may even go so far as to have full-length conversations, out loud, with imagined people while dreaming. Our unconscious body can be completely convinced that a dream is real when we find ourselves "sleep" walking around the house, not knowing the difference between dream time and real life.

All of this occurs as a result of our imagined dreams within the mind. It appears that our physical bodies don't know the difference between that which we have defined as waking life compared to dream time. To the physical body, no separation between these two realities exists. That which we dream about is literally real to our physical body.

Why is it that so many of us have unconsciously decided to accept the limitations of our waking life when, in fact, at least a full quarter of our lives is spent in the world of all possibilities, unlimited potential, and non-linear time? Our ability to dream and visualize all possibilities makes this mindfulness practice of living with a mind wide open and unattached very possible. Perhaps all we must do is live with the updated awareness that life is but a dream—always! There doesn't have to be separation between waking life and dream time. It's simply our choice to open our minds and dream our best dream. Remember, everything is alive, aware, and dreaming.

Many successful athletes use the principle of living with a mind wide open, along with the power of dreaming and visualization, to fulfill their goals. Before scoring the winning point in a NBA basketball game, the result had already been imagined when Kobe Bryant closed his eyes and imagined himself holding the basketball in his hands. He felt the muscle memory of his arms lift the ball into the air, aim it toward the net, and release it, perfectly timed, to swish into the basket. In Kobe's mind, the end result was always inevitable. He saw it before the event even took place in real life. This is the power of an open mind in dream time.

To dream with an open mind and visualize at a level whereby even our bodies feel what is taking place before it occurs is to truly un-attach from all limitations and step into the mindful principle of operating as a no-limits person.

Consider how you would handle a dysfunctional relationship, or any problem in your life for that matter, using the principle of an open mind in dream time. Within the span of thirty seconds, you could shift the way you see a dysfunctional relationship and completely reverse your perspective for the better. You would no longer be stuck in your life's apparent problems; in one simple shift of the mind, you could dream a whole new scenario.

Many of us spend our entire lives feeling stuck, trapped, and attached to the way things seem to be. By living with an open mind, one that accepts the "no limitations" and "life is but a dream" approach to everyday life, we could quickly release all that has tied us down and step into the life we have been imagining. It's time to open up your mind and dream your best dream. It's time to visualize what you want to create for yourself intentionally.

CHAPTER 19

SUGGESTIONS TO CULTIVATE AN OPEN MIND

The journey of a thousand miles begins with one step.
—**Lao Tzu**

Mindfulness practices can assist you with cultivating an open mind and expanding your awareness. It's important to realize, however, that no strategy will be completely successful unless you fully embrace it within yourself and make it a major priority in your life. Here are a few suggestions to kick-start your journey toward cultivating a mind that's open to all possibilities.

Minimize Your Multitasking

Recent studies at Stanford University have found that multitasking is less productive than doing one single task at a time. The research found that people who are regularly bombarded with several streams of electronic information cannot pay attention, recall information, or switch from one job to another as well as those who complete one task at a time.[1] An ancient Hawaiian Huna Kane principle states, "Now is the moment of power."

Consider that when you are not fully present in your mind and body, the energy field surrounding you will shrink. Perhaps you have experienced this first hand. Have you ever been in conversation with someone who's not truly listening to what you're saying? Notice that although he may be there with you in his physical body, his energy field is very small, as he has mentally "left the building." Perhaps you have also been on the other side of this scenario. Can you recall times when you were not fully present to someone speaking to you?

When we mentally wander outside of the present moment, our power decreases and our energy field shrinks. According to the 2010 studies done by Harvard researchers Killingsworth and Gilbert, our mind wanders 47 percent of the time, on average. This means that for almost half the time in your life, you have mentally "left the building" and are not fully present. This isn't always a bad decision. At times, it's important to go inward to daydream and visualize. What's important to know, however, is that when you mentally wander away from the present moment, your energy field shrinks and your charisma decreases.

Alternatively, when you're fully aware and engaged in the present moment, your energy field will expand. When we're fully aware in our mind and body during the moment at hand, we actually become charismatic. Professional speakers, performers, infectious teachers, and leaders know the power that exists in the present moment.

Think about the last time you witnessed an amazing performance or heard an inspiring speech. Chances are, the person on stage was so present in her mind and body that you had no choice but to be drawn into her powerful, present-moment energy. Such is how we become

---

1   https://www.forbes.com/sites/travisbradberry/2014/10/08/multitasking-damages-your-brain-and-career-new-studies-suggest/#2af428e156ee

when we fully engage in the practice of mindfulness. When we show up completely present in the now-moment, our power increases, and we're able to confidently express and perform each task at hand, in union with the entire cosmos. Our presence automatically activates the entire world around us, and what results is the outcome of perfect timing in the present moment. We no longer find ourselves needing to multitask because we know that as we become fully aware of the present moment, all will unfold perfectly on time and deliver to us all that we need, without force.

Multitasking is a major contributor to burnout and stress in our world. With the intention of getting as many things checked off our to-do list as possible, many have convinced themselves that a multitasking approach to life will produce more efficient and rewarding results. As we see in the recent studies conducted at Stanford University, however, people who regularly engage in multitasking struggle with greater levels of burnout and exhaustion and ultimately end up feeling scattered and disorganized.

In fact, multitasking reduces your efficiency and performance because your brain was originally designed to focus on one thing at a time. When you try to do two things at once, your brain lacks the capacity to perform both tasks successfully.[2]

Therefore, doing the dishes, folding the laundry, texting on your phone, cooking a meal, and watching a rerun of your favorite show all at the same time will not produce quality results. In the practice of opening your mind, I encourage you to concentrate on performing one task at a time with focus and intention. To your saboteur, this may seem next to impossible and counterintuitive.

You may even have a career and lifestyle that has become a series of tasks you rush through to try and get it all done, while never really

---

2   http://www.talentsmart.com/articles/Multitasking-Damages-Your-Brain-and-Your-Career,-New-Studies-Suggest-2102500909-p-1.html

arriving at the finish line. According to research and my own experience with the mindfulness practice of opening your mind, I can tell you that you will, ironically, accomplish a lot more at a higher level by breaking things down to one task at a time.

One of my favorite quotes in the *Tao Te Ching* states, "You accomplish more by trying less." Consider how much mental energy you waste by worrying about everything you must somehow accomplish at once. Imagine an alternative lifestyle in which you discipline yourself to focus your energy on the current task at hand—and put aside all other distractions for the time being. Over time, in taking this approach to life, you'll find that your energy level increases, your charisma expands, and that you're actually given all you need, whether it be the right person or the right opportunity arriving perfectly on time.

Anchoring

Another mindfulness practice I offer to you is referred to as anchoring. It's a formal practice to assist in building focus and concentration in your mind. Although this is a formal, intentional practice, you may find that, over time, your anchoring practice naturally seeps into conversations, work tasks, and your overall approach to life.

Just as you would drop a boat anchor into the water to keep a boat secured in one place, so, too, can you train your mind to anchor yourself in the present moment. When we retrain our brain to focus on one thing at a time, new pathways form in the brain, and our concentration levels increase while our stress levels go down.

In the formal practice of anchoring, you simply choose an item to focus your attention on. If you're visual, I recommend concentrating on an image in your mind. A common visual image I use is that of a candle flame burning. If you're not a visual learner, you might instead choose to focus on the inhalation and exhalation of your breath. Notice how both a candle flame and your breathing are constant anchors the mind can focus upon. To formally anchor, set a timer for two to five minutes—or longer, if you choose. Place your full focus on your anchor point. If you choose to focus on your breathing, I suggest that every time you inhale, you also think the thought, "I Am," and every time you exhale, you think the thought, "Now here."

Keep your concentration focused on your anchor point for the entire length of time you have chosen to practice. If you find that your mind begins to wander from the anchor point, simply note what is distracting you and return your focus to the anchor. For example, if I'm focusing on the candle flame and, suddenly, I find myself thinking about my grocery list or even a sensory distraction like a car passing by outside, I simply bottom line note the distraction (e.g., car passing by) and return to my anchor. Over time and with committed dedication to this practice of anchoring, you will find that not only will your mind be less scattered, but you will also accomplish more with a clarity and peace that was only once imagined.

I have found that through daily anchoring practice, my ability to focus on each conversation I engage in during the day has improved, and I'm less likely to miss important information. I've also found that I'm more attuned to the present moment at hand, and as a result, I'm aware of the ideal people arriving into my life at the right time to assist me with what I need. Additionally, I become more in touch with my intuition, which guides me to make the right decisions as I move through my day. Spend some time anchoring every day, and you'll see powerful, positive changes in your life.

The HA Breath

Another very powerful mindfulness practice that can open your mind in a major way is the HA breath. The HA breath originated from an ancient Hawaiian healing lineage called Huna Kane. If you consider the word "Hawaii," you'll note that the sound "HA" is even engrained into this word. HA in Hawaiian translates into the word "breath." Phrases such as aloHA, maHAlo, and oHAna all contain this common sound of "HA." The word "ohana" in Hawaiian is "family" in English. The ancient Hawaiians would often refer to their ohana/family as people who shared the sacred breath together.

My favorite yoga instructor Steve Ross once said, "Breathe until you die." Breath is your life force that flows through your physical body and gives you increased energy; it is, quite simply, your life. The Hawaiians refer to your life force as "mana," while in yoga circles your life force is often referenced as "prana." Chinese medicine calls your life force "chi." No matter what name you give it, your breath is one of the most natural, powerful tools for opening your mind and your awareness.

Many people in North America are chronic shallow breathers. Perhaps we have become this way as a direct result of being so busy—multitasking, stressing, and straining over the constant rush of coming and goings that we have forgotten how to breathe. When tense, the body tightens up and constricts the flow of both blood and breath. This ultimately causes us unease and stress in the physical body, fear in the mental body, and a disconnect between ourselves and an open mind. The HA breathing exercise I now invite you to practice allows you to open your mind and connect back to the present moment. This breath has many layers and meanings; however, in the context of mindfulness, this practice is simply intended to open your mind and increase your awareness.

To formally practice the HA breath, stand with your feet approximately hip-distance apart. Bend your knees slightly and feel your feet press into the ground. Feel a sense of presence and power as you connect to the present moment. Turn your palms up and face them to the sky. To practice the HA breath, you must align your full mental focus with your body and breath.

Set One

Inhale through the nose and place all your focus on the crown (top) of your head. Imagine your water-like breath flowing into your body through the top of your head. As you exhale through the mouth with an audible "HA" sound, similar to that of warming up your hands or fogging a mirror, shift your focus to your feet and imagine your water-like breath streaming all the way down and out through your feet. Repeat four full inhalations and exhalations, keeping your focus on the crown of your head and then at your feet.

Set Two

Next, while you place your entire mental focus on your feet, inhale your water-like breath up from the earth. As you exhale with your HA breath again, shift your attention to the top of your head and watch the water-like breath flow out through the crown of your head. Repeat this round of inhalations and exhalations four times.

Set Three

Place your attention on the top of your head and breathe in your water-like breath through the nose as you bring the breath down into your belly center. As you exhale with an audible HA breath through the mouth, shift your attention to the center of your belly and imagine the water-like breath filling your entire body and the space around you with beautiful energy. Repeat this round four times.

Set Four

In the final set, place your focus on your belly center and breathe in through the nose as your water-like breath fills up the belly. On your exhale breath, out through the mouth with the sound of HA, send the breath out into the world with positive, loving intention. You can choose to send this intentional breath out to the places you're going today or to the people you will meet. You may choose to send this intentional, positive breath to those in your life who have caused you disharmony or, alternatively, to your loved ones. What's important is that you intentionally focus on where you're sending the breath. Repeat this round four times.

It has been said that our physical body has over sixty-thousand energy points. In the ancient yoga tradition, yogis would refer to these points as "nadis," while the Chinese medicine lineage calls these points "meridians." Whatever name you choose, what's important to know is that when we're tense and stressed, these energy points in the body often close up and prevent the flow of energy from moving within us. In contrast, when we're relaxed and breathing with intention, these energy points open up and provide us with newfound energy, clarity, and open-mindedness.

The HA breath is one sure way to increase the flow of energy throughout our body. It's also instrumental in opening our creative mind. Some say that practicing thirty HA breaths in a row can have a similar effect to that of doing hallucinogenic drugs. I have never done drugs, but I can attest that doing thirty HA breaths has a very transformative effect for me. It puts me into a state of open awareness whereby my perceptions of the present moment shift into clarity. Furthermore, the HA breath relaxes my body, especially my shoulders, and gives me an overall feeling of relaxation and stress release. The HA breath also reminds me of the connection between everyone and everything on this planet.

One reason this mindfulness practice works so well is because it connects your intellectual mind with your physical body, and releases the built-up tension from your over-stimulated mind. I invite you to incorporate a regular HA breathing practice in your own life to help you open your mind and release all your built-up tension and anxiety.

Mindfulness Walking

Another strategy for cultivating an open mind is to regularly partake in what is called mindfulness walking. The soul (no pun intended) intention of mindfulness walking is not to pre-plan your experience, but rather to go for a walk in your environment and become an active participant in noticing and objectively observing all that crosses your path. While taking an intentional mindfulness walk, one may purposely use all her senses to deepen her observational experience. For example, you may simply notice the smell of the blooming lilac trees or the colors of the leaves on the ground. Perhaps you hear the sound of birds singing their authentic tune or feel the texture of a tree while reaching out to feel its bark.

Wherever you are and whatever you notice, attempt to experience it all from a place of non-judgment, labeling, or attachment. Become an appreciator of all the life that surrounds you and take note of each moment that awakens before you as you place one foot in front of the other. Mindfulness walking is a great strategy to change the energy within you. This can be an especially effective practice to release pent up energy and stress that has accumulated in your mind and body. It can also awaken a deeper sense of acceptance toward all that crosses your path. When we let go of judgment and move into a place of full acceptance, our minds remain open and we may even begin to feel a sense of compassion and connection to all that surrounds us.

New Experiences

Another way to cultivate an open mind is to intentionally commit to exploring new experiences. Whether it's reading a book in a subject area or genre you normally wouldn't choose or creating a new piece of artwork, practicing yoga, learning a new instrument, enrolling in a new course of study, or taking a trip to an unexplored destination, the practice of trying new things and experiencing the unfamiliar awakens us to new levels of awareness.

If you're intentional in your pursuit to explore new aspects of this rich and abundant world, your mind will open to new levels of awareness and creativity. Take the time to open your mind and step outside of your regular routines. As you open your mind to new experiences, you may find that you have more energy, a new lease on life, and a feeling of release from all the mundane tasks that clutter your life. Consider making a list of twenty things you have not yet tried and set out to experience some of them over the next month.

Free Writing

For the past three years, I've taken half an hour almost every morning to free write. With a pen in my hand and a scribbler in front of me, I follow these guidelines to open my mind and write:

1. Set no limits on what to write about.
2. Keep your pen moving. Don't stop to think about what you just wrote.
3. Take the pressure off yourself. No one else will read these pages, so write whatever comes into your mind, with no restrictions or reservations.
4. Reject the rule that it must make sense. Our minds can become a storehouse of crowded thoughts that bog us down and prevent us from being in the present moment. Use this time to dump all that's streaming through your mind and write it down. As you do this, you'll release all the clutter taking up space in your mind. Nothing you write on these pages has to make sense. Just let the words flow out.
5. Allow! Give yourself permission to pour out whatever needs to be written down on the page. We spend enough time in

our lives following rules and conforming to the expectations of both outside opinions and our own internal dialogue. Allow yourself to fully engage in your free writing with all possibility set before you; no limits are placed on what you write about here.

Free writing is a wonderful way to open your mind and release any attachments to how things should be. Through this practice, you'll become more present and aware of what is actually going on underneath the surface of your thoughts. You may also find, upon completion of a free writing session, that you feel and experience new-found space within you. Many people say free writing sessions enhance their feelings of creativity and minimize the stress that once took up space in their minds and bodies. I suggest taking some time to try a free writing session and discover what emerges for you. After all, free writing is free of charge. What do you have to lose?

Surround Yourself with Inspiration

Another suggestion to cultivate an open mind is to regularly surround yourself with inspirational objects, images, and people. This could include printing out positive quotes that stimulate an open mind and posting them in places you frequently visit (e.g., the walls of your home or office). While driving, you might choose to listen to an inspiring audio book instead of tuning in to breaking news stories, which often lower our energy levels.

Setting up time in your schedule to connect with people who make you feel good and inspire you to think outside the box is another way to practice this mindfulness strategy. Or, consider attending monthly mastermind group meetings to inspire yourself with new perspectives and ideas. For those not familiar with this concept, a mastermind group is typically a small group of inspiring individuals who commit to meeting on a regular basis to brainstorm new ideas and facilitate innovative thinking. The group holds each other accountable to pushing past individual limits.

Other ideas on how to surround yourself with inspiration might include hiring a life coach, cooking a new recipe, reading a new book or magazine, watching inspiring videos and live lectures, and going to see live theater or music. I invite you to make your own list, which you can regularly refer to, so that your mind continues to expand, open, and flourish.

Meditate

Paramahansa Yogananda writes, "By the power of meditation, you can direct the inexhaustible power of your mind to accomplish what you desire and to guard every door against failure." Those who know how to open their mind and focus it intentionally through the practice of meditation can easily connect to the creative power that is always available to guide and lead one to exactly what she needs.

You can conduct the practice of meditation in many forms. It can be as simple as calming all the senses and focusing on your breath (much like the anchoring practice outlined earlier), or mindful walking, eating, yoga, jogging, swimming, or even biking. Meditation is not so much about the act of doing but about how you are *being* while you're doing. Meditation is an intentional focusing of the mind to relax and become an observer of the present moment so that we can listen to our intuition. When we learn how to listen to our intuition, we're given all the wisdom we need to create the life we desire.

Our mind and body are in direct relationship with each other. The mind plays host to our decision making, while the body hosts our intuition and gut feelings. Although our mind is great at making decisions and taking action, many times, it dominates our attention with its continuous, internal chatter and cuts off the connection to our intuition. When overstimulated, our mind can quickly cloud our awareness and lead us into patterns of overthinking, overanalyzing, and over-stressing. I often think of the connection between my mind and my intuitive body as two partners in a relationship. When my mind plays the role of the "over-talker" in the relationship, rarely listening to what my internal intuition has to say, I find myself out of balance and disconnected.

In contrast to our busy, chattering mind, our intuition is our inner-gut knowing, our connection to creativity, and our wisdom. We'll explore the dynamic relationship between mind and intuition further in the following pages. However, for the purpose of explaining meditation here, it's important to know that your intuition holds all your wisdom and inspiration and ultimately knows what is best for you in every situation. Intuition, essentially, is your inner compass. Although it holds all wisdom and clarity, very rarely in our day-to-day life do we take the time to listen to our intuition. Instead, our mind rambles on with all sorts of information and knowledge that may or may not be relevant to the situation at hand.

In the practice of meditation, we learn to refocus and train the thinking mind to become an active listener to our intuition. We work toward finding balance in the relationship between the active thinking mind and our intuition. What's important is learning how to distinguish the difference between an overactive, thinking mind and intuitive wisdom. The overactive, thinking mind tends to be accompanied by feelings of stress, busyness, and a whole lot of information. Our intuition on the other hand is often experienced as a deep, peaceful feeling within us. It often resonates as an unspoken truth within our consciousness. When the mind and the body's intuition are in harmony, we experience balance. We no longer worry about life's unending pressures and demands, but instead remain poised, centered, and connected to internal clarity.

To hear our intuition clearly, we must be willing to quiet the mind, focus inward, pay attention, and be present to the wisdom that often whispers to us through silent, inner-knowings. Our intuition can only communicate with us when we are fully present. Though it often communicates with us through a deep inner knowing, it can also speak to us in the form of peaceful feelings or through signs and symbols in our imagination. It's the part that silently guides us toward what we know, deep down, is truthful, resonant, and right.

In the practice of meditation, we become more and more attuned to listening, both formally and informally, to the intuitive place within us, and then we grow bold in taking action based on the cues we are given. We teach our thinking mind to pay attention and listen to the truth, which is only found in the present-moment awareness within ourselves. To trust yourself and act on your intuition through this dynamic practice of meditation is a sure way to open your mind and live fully engaged in the world.

Visualization

The practice of visualization is another effective method for opening the mind. With visualization, the mind and body must work together to achieve a desired outcome. The body provides the active use of all five senses, while the mind offers its ability to focus upon imagination and creativity.

For example, in a visualization with the intention of relaxing, one may close his eyes, connect to the feeling and sound of his breath, and then imagine himself sitting in a beautiful garden. As he allows his imagination to create the scenario of a garden, he may start feeling the temperature in the garden, a gentle breeze on his skin, or the smell of flowers on the trees that surround him. He may also hear the sound of a gentle stream running by. As his senses awaken and connect with his imagination, it becomes as if the visualizer is actually experiencing a real-life garden.

Visualization exercises are effective because the body doesn't know the difference between real, waking life and dream time. As Principle 1 of mindfulness states, "Everything begins as an inner dream." Through visualization, not only can we experience the lucidity of our imagination, but we can learn how to open our mind and visualize the outcomes we want—before they even occur in our waking life.

Athletes, innovators, and performers know the secret magic that exists in the practice of visualization. Many successful outcomes—including winning goals, life-changing inventions, and world records—were achieved through the power of internal visualization.

Take some time to try a visualization exercise on your own. Many guided visualizations are offered online, and you can find one there to help you get started. Alternatively, you can begin a visualization practice right now by simply closing your eyes, taking a few deep breaths and focusing your mind on a specific outcome you would like to achieve. Use all your senses and imagination to awaken within you what it feels like to achieve the desired outcome. Take your time with this and only open your eyes when you feel that you've internally experienced what you desire. Expect to now see this outcome manifest in your external world in the days ahead.

By practicing visualization, you'll become even more attuned to mindfulness Principle 3: Open Your Mind. You'll realize that there are no limits to what is possible, and that an open mind can produce transformative results in your life. As Wayne Dyer suggests, "You'll see it when you believe it."

Ask Why and Be Curious

Early on, many of us learned to discount our curiosity and follow the directions of authority figures, including teachers, parents, and community leaders. Our natural curiosity about why things are the way they are was often downplayed and discouraged. As children, how often were our questions dismissed by, "That's just the way it is"? Notice that this learned pattern of neglecting to ask why continues from childhood into our high school and college years, when we rarely ask questions about what we're learning and, instead, regurgitate the memorized data we've been given by our teachers. This pattern extends into adulthood and is known as the "top-down" approach, whereby top executives create policies and protocols without giving their employees the opportunity to question decisions.

Ultimately, this approach of little to no questioning often takes precedence in our society. It then breeds an unspoken discouragement of creativity, with a focus instead on following rules, protocol, and playing it safe. It's ironic, therefore, that the most successful corporate businesses and leaders are those who've broken from the societal norm to become top innovators—all because they never stopped asking why. While the rest of us took a back seat, the true leaders and creators refused to conform.

We can learn much from these rare characters who continue to ask questions and push limits. In fact, consider this another intentional mindfulness practice. To open your mind to all possibility is to ask the deep and meaningful questions that come across your mind. To truly wonder and approach life with the question of why is a bold and powerful stance. In so doing, not only do we grow and expand our mental capability, but we also realize that the only things stopping us from becoming all we could be are the attachments and limitations we've adopted from societal conditioning.

The great poet Rumi writes, "Sell your cleverness and purchase your bewilderment." As you explore and implement Principle 3 into your life, I encourage you to approach each moment with awe and bewilderment. From the flower blossoming before your eyes to the baby learning to take her first steps, be in a state of complete and utter openness. Soak up each moment and refuse to take life for granted.

While writing this chapter, I learned that a dear friend and colleague had passed away. He was a young man of forty-eight years old. He left his wife and two children behind after suffering a heart attack on a road trip to a basketball tournament. Dale was a man of many talents and lived his life to the fullest degree. He always volunteered his time and energy to help in the community and lived each moment to the fullest. As I reflect on Dale's passing, I'm once again reminded that life is too short to spend our time in apprehension and fear. For when you sell your cleverness and escape your overly analytical ego, you come to see that creativity and expansion is your birth right. Go forward and be open to all that shows up on your path, for the universe wants to reveal its secrets to you.

CHAPTER 20

AN OPEN MIND PREVENTS DISEASE

Belief creates the actual fact.
—**William James**

T here have been many medical studies regarding the placebo effect. The placebo effect is a beneficial effect produced by a placebo drug or treatment that cannot be attributed to the properties of the placebo itself and must, therefore, be due to the patient's belief in that treatment. Knowing that the placebo effect does, in fact, produce healing results based on a patient's belief system, I would further argue that we can heal our bodies from illness by shifting our inner beliefs.

To conclude this section on Principle 3: Open Your Mind, I would like to share an anecdote I first learned through Wayne Dyer. Perhaps this short story will further remind you of how important and powerful it can be to cultivate an open mind. It may even prevent you from illness.

Miss Beatrice, the church organist, was in her eighties and had never been married. She was admired for her sweetness and kindness to all. One afternoon, the pastor came to call on her, and she showed him into her quaint sitting room. She invited him to have a seat while she prepared tea. As he sat facing her old Hammond organ, the young minister noticed a glass bowl sitting on top of it. The bowl was filled with water, and in the water floated, of all things, a condom.

When she returned with tea and scones, they chatted. The pastor tried to stifle his curiosity about the bowl of water and its strange floater, but soon it got the better of him, and he could no longer resist. "Miss Beatrice," he said, "I wonder if you would tell me about this?" He pointed to the bowl.

"Oh, yes," she replied, "isn't it wonderful? I was walking through the park a few months ago, and I found this little package on the ground. The directions said to place it on the organ and keep it wet and that it would prevent the spread of disease. Do you know, I haven't had the flu all winter?"

This humorous tale demonstrates the ultimate portrayal of what can take place when we have a mind open to everything and attached to nothing. Those who consistently pursue a life fully open to all possibilities will meet with true success. To be mindful is to fully open your mind and wake up to the limitless potential each moment offers.

Consider the challenging areas in your life. Can you open your mind and find a new way to look at the situation at hand? What would your life potentially be like if you changed the way you've been viewing this challenge? Principle 3 requires you to fully take responsibility for your thinking and your approach to life. You have the power to decide how you want to look at the world around you. With an open mind, you'll meet with much abundance and freedom. Such is the standard when you are living a mindful life.

CHAPTER 21

LIVING AWARENESS

What is necessary to change a person
is to change his awareness of himself.
—Abraham Maslow

In 1906, psychologist William James wrote, "We are only making use of a small part of our possible mental and physical resources." In 1963, journalist Lowell Thomas noted the following in the forward to Dale Carnegie's famous self-help book *How to Win Friends and Influence People*: "The average person develops only ten percent of his latent mental ability." As I write this book on mindfulness, I'm left asking, "What are the missing resources within us and how can we tap into this undiscovered potential?"

Principle 4: Live Mind-Fully Aware

Mindfulness Principle 4 suggests that to be mindfully aware is to operate at a full 100 percent capacity. To access our "full" operating system, we must be in touch with all aspects of who we truly are. In Principle 4, we learn that most people in our world are only consciously operating in one-third of who they truly are. To become fully aware of the other two-thirds of who you are is a powerful asset in navigating through life with deeper clarity and understanding. It has an almost magical aspect to it.

I often reference this principle as the "big kahuna" step to making sense of mindfulness because within it exists a fundamental blueprint and explanation to help us understand who we truly are and how we can better function as human beings in this physical world. In my opinion, this is the principle that holds the greatest potential and ultimate pay off for those who fully comprehend and concretely apply it to their lives.

Over the past fifteen years, as a life coach, healer, and teacher, I have come to see Principle 4 as my foundation for all healing success and inner peace. If you're able to comprehend and apply Principle 4, not only will you be engaged in the practice of living mindfully, but you'll also be living at a level of life most people only dream of.

To reveal Principle 4: Live Mind-Fully Aware, you must first understand that your mind consists of three different parts: the conscious mind, unconscious mind, and higher self. As I mentioned, the majority of us live our lives consciously aware of only one of these three aspects. To become mindfully aware, we must understand all three parts of our mind and work toward getting them to work together.

In an attempt to share this principle with you, I will spend some time explaining these three aspects and outlining their attributes. Following this, I'll demonstrate how these three aspects work together, and how you can intentionally use them to achieve a successful mindfulness practice in your everyday life.

CHAPTER 22

THE CONSCIOUS MIND

Sometimes it's the smallest decisions
that can change your life forever.
—**Keri Russell**

The first part of our mind we'll discuss in relation to Principle 4 is a very familiar aspect for most. It's the part of our mind we engage with most often—in fact, almost all the time. To experience it right now, first hand, I would like to play a game with you. I'm going to present you with a few scenarios and options, and I want you to make a choice based on your first instinct.

Scenario #1
You are going on a vacation. Would you rather:
    A. Take a trip to a hot, tropical island and relax,
    B. Or go on a more active vacation, with sightseeing and planned activities?

Scenario #2

You are listening to your car radio in a very remote area, and only two radio stations come in clearly. Would you rather:

A. Listen to old country songs from the 1950s,

B. Or listen to pop/rock songs from the 1990s?

Scenario #3

You have already decided to go for a workout. Would you rather:

A. Take a yoga class,

B. Or go for a swim?

Notice that in all these scenarios, along with almost every other moment of your waking life, you are *making decisions*. This ability is powered by the first aspect to your mind in the Live Mind-Fully Aware Principle, the aspect I'll refer to as the conscious mind.

The main function of the conscious mind is to make decisions. Researchers at Cornell University found that people make an average of 226.7 decisions a day about food alone.[3] It has been suggested that we typically make over 60,000 decisions a day in our conscious minds. From the food we eat, to the clothes we wear, to the way we deal with people, our conscious mind is at work in every decision. Most of us spend the majority of our time operating in the conscious mind.

It's important to note that our decision making is influenced by various sources. Some are internal, others external. These sources may include our past experiences, personal likes and dislikes, the opinions of others, and even our inner-saboteur conditioning. Notice that whenever we make a decision, it automatically generates a pattern in our lives. For example, if we make a decision (influenced by our saboteur conditioning) that suggests we will never find true love, we may, indeed,

---

3   Brian Wansink and Jeffrey Sobal (2007), "Mindless Eating: The 200 Daily Food Decisions We Overlook," *Environment and Behavior* 39:1 (2007): 106-123.

never attract true love—until we make a new decision. However, if we make a decision in our conscious mind that affirms true love is on the way and here to stay, we will most likely attract love into our lives.

The conscious mind is often referred to as our intellectual part. It's our central control center, deciding what we want and how we're going to make it happen. Many times, the decisions we make are determined by our inner assumptions and the beliefs we've been holding on to. Other times, our decisions are made by impulse and intuition. What's important to remember is that this central control center is really where the decisions that shape our lives are made (both consciously and unconsciously).

It's in the conscious mind that we decide how our lives are going to be and what we want to create: What type of work do you currently find yourself in? Who are the people with whom you have associated yourself? How do you spend your free time? What clothes did you decide to wear today? How do you style your hair? What type of car do you drive?

As you consider how these aspects show up in your life, you may now realize they all began as decisions made in the control center, your conscious mind. This awareness is the first step to becoming mindfully aware—it's to understand that our conscious mind is consistently making decisions, and these decisions generate patterns that then determine how our lives unfold. Be aware of your thinking and the decisions you make. For, your current thinking will become your future. Remember, thoughts become reality.

CHAPTER 23

THE UNCONSCIOUS MIND

The conscious mind determines the actions, the unconscious mind determines the reactions; and the reactions are just as important as the actions.

—**E. Stanley Jones**

I now invite you to close your eyes and focus on the following instructions: Recall the last time you had a really big belly laugh. Can you remember where you were, who you were with, and what was taking place? Even if you can't remember an exact time that you had a big belly laugh, I'd like you to focus your attention on belly laughing. Try to feel the energy of belly laughing and even put your body into that state. Go ahead. Close your eyes and try it now.

What happened? Were you able to connect to the feeling of belly laughing? How did your body feel as you connected to that memory and the feeling of laughing? Right now, if you dare, start belly laughing out loud. Even with nothing to laugh about, just try to laugh out loud. Now, increase it to double the intensity until you feel a shift in your body's energy level. Can you feel it? If you haven't tried any of these activities yet, you may be operating exclusively in your conscious, intellectual mind right now. As I mentioned earlier, this is where most of us live. To become mindfully aware, we must be willing to engage with the other two parts of self. Unless you take intentional action right now and try these laughing exercises, you'll find it harder to connect with this second aspect of who you are as we discuss it. So, go ahead. Try imagining or actually laughing out loud until you feel the emotion.

If you did make contact with the feeling of belly laughing, you just met and connected with the next aspect of your mind in the Live Mind-Fully Aware Principle: the unconscious mind. The unconscious mind is a dynamic and multi-layered aspect of who we are. Although this part of our mind is in constant operation, many of us don't consider its function or understand how to successfully utilize it to improve our lives. To fully understand this mysterious aspect of who you are, I'd like to share some of the unconscious mind's attributes. It's important to note here that the unconscious mind is multi-dimensional. Therefore, capturing its entire essence is next to impossible in one book. Even so, I will offer you as much as I can so that you might begin developing a relationship with this important part of who you are.

CHAPTER 24

ATTRIBUTES OF THE UNCONSCIOUS MIND

Man's task is to become conscious of the contents that press upwards from the unconscious.

—Carl Jung

It Holds All Memory

The unconscious mind holds all of your memories. It's like an ultimate hard drive, with unlimited terabyte space available to store all the events of your life. The unconscious mind remembers everything that has ever happened to you. It can recall where you have been, who you were with, what you were wearing, how you felt, what you learned, and every other sensory detail, all the way back to your earliest days of life.

Recall the belly laugh experiment. Were you able to feel a belly laugh? As soon as I gave you the instruction, your unconscious mind began searching its memory bank for the feeling and memory of laughing. Were you able to re-experience that sensation?

It has been said that the conscious mind (the part of us that makes decisions) can only retain approximately two minutes of memory. The unconscious mind, on the other hand, can recall a lifetime. The unconscious mind can even remember details your conscious mind is unaware of. The unconscious mind is like eyes at the back of your head. For example, right now, your unconscious mind is, at a certain level, remembering the colors of the place you're in. It's also absorbing the smells around you and registering the way your body feels as you read this book. Until I pointed this out, you may not have been consciously aware of the colors around you, the smell of the space you're in, or the feeling in your body. The unconscious mind, however, is always retaining and storing memory.

It Runs the Body

As you read, you're not consciously thinking about the air moving in and out through your nostrils or the powerful organ continuously thumping to spread blood throughout your body. You are also unaware that your hair and fingernails are growing. This is because your body is animated by your unconscious mind, not your conscious thinking mind. It's your unconscious mind that remembers to take care of your bodily functions because it holds all memory. Imagine if your conscious mind was responsible for every breath. It would be next to impossible for it to remember each breath you needed to take. It's the unconscious mind that automatically remembers to breathe and, at the same time, remembers to run the rest of your body, too.

The unconscious mind is essentially your physical body. All memories are stored in the physical body. How do we know this? Have you ever observed the physiology of someone who didn't get enough sleep the night before? What does her body language convey—perhaps yawning, shoulders slouched, and eyes half opened? Her body language conveys the memory of the previous night. Have you ever experienced someone who, without saying anything out loud, convinced you he was down and out? What did his body language communicate—maybe shoulders slouched forward, head dropped down low, and lips turned downward? Compare this physical body to someone full of joy and happiness. Her chest may be puffed up, her head is held high, and the corners of her lips are lifted. Our physical body and physiology hold the underlying truth of who we are.

As a yoga instructor, I often deduce the kind of day my students are having by simply observing their physical posture and body language. The yoga student who has had a busy, stressful day will most likely wobble around in the balancing postures and may even have a difficult time being still and present. At the same time, I can pinpoint the students who are experiencing happiness and balance in their lives by the way they hold themselves in class. Their chests are puffed out in celebration, and their faces contain bright, contagious smiles.

Because the body is the unconscious mind and stores all memory, our physical bodies hold the information about what's going on in our lives. Medical intuitive Carolyn Myss writes, "Your biography becomes your biology." It's important to understand that our memory is in our physiology. Our past experiences are stored in our bones, so to speak.

It Is Literal

The unconscious mind is literal, taking everything at face value, with no filter system. For example, self-deprecating humor we sometimes engage in will be interpreted by the unconscious mind as a face-value truth. An unintentional, humorous thought or comment, such as, "I'm so stupid," gets interpreted by the unconscious mind as literal truth. Unlike the conscious mind, which can make a filtered decision that self-deprecating humor is intended to be a joke, the unconscious mind takes everything as truth and stores it as memory in our body.

Just last night, I was watching a comedian on Netflix who began his talk with the comment, "You are not special, even though you think you are." His comment was intended to be a joke. My conscious mind, the decision-making part of me, was able to filter this statement and realize it was a joke; however, my unconscious mind took the comment at face value and stored it as a memory, assuming, "I am not special." To reprogram this memory, I must consciously tell my unconscious mind that the comedian was only joking and, in fact, I am special.

Have you ever awakened to a sore neck? At a conscious level, you may simply decide you slept on it the wrong way. However, to the unconscious mind, you may consider addressing the following question: "Who is my pain in the neck?" Remember, your body holds all memory and is extremely literal. One of the main languages of our bodies, aka the unconscious mind, is sensation. The body attempts to communicate with our conscious thinking mind through the language of sensation and feeling. This is why we often feel a rumbling in our stomachs when we're hungry. It's the body's way of reminding us to eat. In the case of a stiff neck, you may want to internally ask your neck, "What memory is associated with this sensation?"

I have become accustomed to speaking with my physical body and learning how to listen to its inner wisdom. Knowing my unconscious mind holds all my memory—to an extent my conscious mind might not even comprehend—I've come to trust that the sensations and feelings in my body are cues to pay attention to my unconscious mind.

One morning, I woke up with a stiff neck. On that particular morning, I internally asked my neck what it was trying to communicate. Within a few moments of internal listening, I was given a memory of someone in my life against whom I was holding a grudge. This person had literally become a "pain in my neck." Upon receiving this insight from my unconscious mind, I consciously made it my intention to clear up the issue with this particular person. Within a few days of addressing the situation with this pain-in-the-neck person, the physical pain in my neck subsided, proving how literally our unconscious-body mind operates.

Consider how common sayings such as "Listen to your heart" or "I have a gut feeling" originated in reference to the unconscious-body-mind connection within us. Our body has literal wisdom to share with us. The issue is, because most of us live predominately in our conscious mind, we often neglect to listen to our unconscious-body mind. In the practice of mindfulness, it becomes essential that our conscious mind intentionally takes the role of "listener" in its relationship with our unconscious mind. In doing so, we can better align with our inner body wisdom and consciously become aware of how to live our lives in the best way possible. Using the internal-memory wisdom of our unconscious mind, we attune ourselves to what is true and learn to act on the wisdom we are given.

In her book *The Magic Path of Intuition*, Florence Shinn shares the story of a woman who owned a beautiful set of pearls. The woman had great wealth but always spoke about her "lack" and would repeatedly say, "Someday I'll have to eat those pearls." This saying was intended to be a joke, a comment on how her life was too good to be true. Upon regularly hearing this statement, however, the woman's unconscious mind delivered exactly what she was asking for. Her fortune vanished, and she had to sell her pearls to buy food.

Another example of how literally the unconscious mind operates occurred when a young man jokingly used the phrase, "I am so sick and tired of having to do everything around here." He used this phrase as a joke to respond to his coworkers when they asked how his job was going. Ironically, the man had a wonderful job that didn't require strenuous effort on his part. Much to his surprise, the young man found himself becoming overly tired and run down on a regular basis. This eventually led to an illness that caused him to take a sick leave from work. As he pondered the cause of his illness, it occurred to the young man that he'd received what he had been asking for on an unconscious level. Now, when asked how he is doing, the young man responds with, "I am well." Since changing his response, the young man's health has returned, and he is back to work at his fulfilling job.

What's encouraging to know about the literal nature of the unconscious mind is that once it's in harmony with the conscious thinking mind, we can consciously begin creating the life we want, using our thoughts, words, and actions. This mindful wisdom dates back to 1897 when a London periodical printed the outline of a sermon intended for children; it presented the acronym WATCH to convey a powerful mindfulness practice:

W: Watch your Words.
A: Watch your Actions.
T: Watch your Thoughts.
C: Watch your Companions. (I would also like to add Character.)
H: Watch your Habits.

Frank Outlaw, the late president of Bi-Lo stores, a successful supermarket chain in the United States, wrote the following:

Watch your thoughts, they become words;
watch your words, they become actions;
watch your actions, they become habits;
watch your habits, they become character;
watch your character, for it becomes your destiny.

Knowing that the unconscious mind takes everything literally, a successful mindfulness practice begins when we consciously act on the advice given by both the 1897 London sermon and Frank Outlaw's wisdom. Listen to your unconscious mind and you'll acquire important wisdom that will help shape your life's journey.

It Hosts Our Emotions and Feelings

According to the Center for Addiction and Mental Health, one in five people experience a mental health or addiction problem in their lives. The statistics released regarding cases of mental health, anxiety, and depression show an alarming increase in new diagnoses. We are seeing increased levels of anxiety and depression among all age levels and in all areas of our society, from school children to adults and even senior citizens. You may ask, "Why is there such an increase in anxiety and depression in our culture?"

The mental health epidemic cannot be easily explained; however, by considering the function of our unconscious mind, we may gain an understanding of why we're seeing these alarming trends—in anxiety and depression in particular. An awareness of the unconscious mind's role may also provide possible solutions for such conditions.

We live in a culture that has collectively agreed on rules and ways of being that suggest, "The harder you work, the more successful and valued you will be." Our culture tends to believe that multitasking is the only efficient approach, the only way to accomplish all we need to get done. Furthermore, our culture has an unspoken, collective belief that the public display of certain emotions is weak and unacceptable. Does any of this sound familiar to you? Has it occurred to you that perhaps we're living in a time where our intellectual, conscious, decision-making minds are being influenced by a collective, saboteur mentality?

In addition, it seems that many give top priority to their intellectual minds, never truly listening to the unconscious part of who they are.

If we buy into the collective saboteur mindset—"The harder we work, the more successful we will be," or, "The more money we acquire, the greater our true worth"—we not only end up putting a lot of pressure on ourselves, but we also program our unconscious-body mind and memory to *believe* these collective decisions. As a result, our physical bodies tighten up from increased stress levels and constricted blood flow. This tension can lead to heart attack, sick leave, anxiety, depression, and an overall disconnect.

To add to this equation, another attribute that holds great importance is the understanding that the unconscious mind is host to our emotions and feelings. Earlier, when I asked you to belly laugh—if you actually tried it—you felt the emotion of happiness come over you. If I asked you to recall a memory of the last time you cried, with some intentional focus, you would feel the same feelings triggered as when you first had the experience.

Our unconscious mind is directly connected to our feelings. It has been said that emotion is literally energy in motion. For example, when we have a good cry, what takes place on the unconscious level of our being is that energy simply flows through our physical body. The emotional energy flow attempts to move us through the experiences we're having. Have you ever noticed that after a good cry, you are left with a feeling of spaciousness and clarity? It's much the same after you let yourself feel and express anger. At the end of a full, emotional flow of anger through our body, we return to our natural state of being.

I find it very counterintuitive that our society has collectively agreed to suppress certain feelings and emotions. From a very early age, many of us were told that crying is weak or that being angry is something to avoid or "deal with." Consider what happens on an unconscious level to an emotion (energy in motion), such as crying, when our conscious mind decides we're not allowed to feel it. If crying is simply energy in motion, and we suppress or stop the energy from flowing, where does it go? The memory, along with the feeling, gets stuck in the cells of our body. It gets trapped in the unconscious-body mind, and if not expressed fully, it will gradually turn into inflammation and constriction in the physical body. In turn, this will eventually result in physical "dis-ease." Much of the disease in our body, on the unconscious level, is caused by a suppression of the feelings and emotions denied the opportunity to flow through us in an outward expression.

Upon closer examination, perhaps part of the anxiety and depression outbreak in our world today is a result of accepting our culture's message that we are not allowed to feel our feelings and must stuff them down. When energy gets trapped or stuffed, so to speak, it has to find another way to express and release. A tight chest, anxiety in the gut, a general, unexplained sadness, and all the other symptoms of depression and anxiety can be traced back to a suppression of feelings and emotions.

The interesting thing is, as a society, we tend to override our unconscious mind even further by choosing to believe that something is wrong with those who claim to be depressed and anxious. Instead of creating the space to simply listen, without judgment, allowing each other to express anxious and depressed emotions freely, our society has programmed us to turn to medications and pharmaceutical drugs. Consequently, this creates isolation and further blocks the energy in our body from flowing.

Therefore, it's important to know that the unconscious mind plays host to our emotions and feelings. In a successful mindfulness practice, it becomes essential to allow yourself to feel and let all the emotions you're feeling flow through you. When we allow our emotions to naturally flow through us, we're no longer stuck, holding on to stuffed, unprocessed memories. It takes a lot of effort to keep emotions trapped in the body. It also becomes much more difficult to be in our own true power, because we end up focusing our unconscious attention on repressing unexpressed feelings, instead of being free to feel and respond to what is taking place in the present-moment reality. Mindfulness requires giving yourself permission to express all you're feeling in the present moment, without restriction.

It Operates in Patterns, Symbols, and Repetition

Consider the processes you use to retain all you want to remember. It's through the use of patterns, symbols, and repetition, right? Our unconscious mind uses symbols and patterns, along with repetition, to store all memory.

When I was in grade school, I remember my mother keeping me home from school one day when she learned I wasn't doing well in math class. I had been struggling with multiplication equations and was failing all my math quizzes. For an entire day, my mother and I reviewed multiplication flash cards repeatedly until the answers became next to automatic in my brain. I remember returning to class the following day and acing every multiplication quiz from that day forward.

The unconscious mind responds very favorably to repetition. Have you ever listened to a repetitive song on the radio and several days later still find yourself singing the catchy parts? How about the regular routines that become so automatic you no longer realize that you do them? Have you ever driven to work but couldn't quite recall how you arrived there in one piece? How about the time you ate breakfast and a few hours later couldn't recall what you ate? To the unconscious mind, the tasks we do repetitively turn into regular patterns and habits. After driving to work day in and day out for several days in a row, you no longer have to consciously think about getting to and from work. Your unconscious mind takes over and automatically delivers you the pattern. The same goes for eating breakfast, brushing your teeth, putting on your clothes, and so on. Once we've trained our unconscious-memory mind to perform a specific task through the use of constant repetition, we no longer need to focus consciously on doing it.

When we truly want to become aware of the present moment, we need to approach each moment with a beginner's mind. We must consciously refocus on the tasks we're performing with the same intention we held when we set out to do the task the first time. This is why being present in the moment to each task you're performing is so crucial. If you're mindfully eating a meal, you must make the conscious decision to take your unconscious mind off autopilot and become consciously aware of the tastes and textures you're experiencing with each bite. You must even become aware of how your body responds to the food you're putting into it. When we align our conscious and unconscious minds in the present moment and deliberately take our lives off autopilot, we tap into a very powerful mindfulness practice. The simple, mundane tasks of everyday life are no longer to-do list tasks, but are intentionally performed and enjoyed. We're consciously able to work directly with our unconscious mind to ensure that we're intentionally aware of how we interact with each passing moment.

Beyond repetition, the unconscious mind also uses patterns and symbols. It can interpret symbols through the use of collective memory. For example, through past experience, the unconscious mind knows that the color red at a stoplight means stop; it knows green means go. Through stored memory, the unconscious mind knows that the symbol for hot is red and cold is blue. We often take for granted symbols and their associated meanings because our unconscious mind processes the meanings from its memory bank so quickly and automatically.

Many times, we don't actually see the "writing on the wall," so to speak, because we're concentrated in our conscious minds, making decisions based on many other factors and distractions. Consciously paying attention to the signs and symbols around us can be a powerful mindfulness practice. Just yesterday, I was having lunch with my wife at one of our favorite juice bars. I had been there several times and never noticed the positive quotes written on the wall. This particular time, however, my wife pointed out that one of the quotes said, "Healthy self = heal thy self." As soon as I saw this quote, I was reminded of my recent choice to start eating healthier. It was a direct affirmation from the universe. As my conscious mind woke up to what my unconscious mind already knew to be true, I was reassured that my new way of eating was a good choice. The writing was literally on the wall.

When we're paying attention, signs and symbols are all around us, encouraging us and supporting us. You will realize, by making sense of your mindfulness practice, all things are connected. At the unconscious level of awareness, the signs and symbols to support this truth are all around us—if we consciously choose to pay attention.

It Is Like a Little Child

Consider the energy of small children. They're always seeking pleasure and are curious about everything around them. Much like a young child, our unconscious mind is drawn to pleasure and play. The unconscious mind always reverts to what it deems is the most pleasurable, fun memory we've associated with an event, experience, or decision. Much like a child, the unconscious mind is drawn to the shiniest objects. What you decide is fun and pleasurable on a conscious, decision-making level will soon become the automatic pattern the unconscious mind gravitates toward. This is how both good and bad habits form. We'll explore this aspect in greater depth in the next chapter.

Signs and Symbols Exercise

For the rest of the day, pay close attention to the various signs and symbols you see around you. Notice that everything has an inner message to share. What's the world around you trying to convey in the present moment? How is the message connected to your life? Perhaps you see an unexpected flower shooting up between a crack in the sidewalk and are reminded that all things are possible. Maybe you see a billboard sign as you're driving to work that states, "Don't give up," and in that moment, you're reminded that everything is working out on time. Or, perhaps a voice on the radio offers you the exact advice you were looking for, and all you did was turn on the radio at the right time. Our unconscious mind operates on the symbolic level. Start paying attention to this amazing aspect of who you are, and you may be quite amazed at the results that appear.

CHAPTER 25

UNDERSTANDING HABITS

We first make our habits, and then our habits make us.
—John Dryden

It's Friday evening, and you have just finished a long week of work. You arrive home and have a free night ahead of you. You decide to pour yourself a glass of wine, kick back, relax, and enjoy the beginning of your weekend. Before too long, you've finished your enjoyable glass of wine. Without hesitation, you decide to refill your glass and have another. As the evening progresses, you find yourself finishing the entire bottle of wine (and maybe even moving on to the next bottle or more). The next morning arrives, and you have trouble getting out of bed. You tell yourself you will never drink wine again. However, the next weekend arrives, and once again you find yourself doing it all over. It has become a habit.

A habit is an acquired behavior pattern that is regularly followed until it becomes almost involuntary and unconscious. Habits are formed and exist in the unconscious mind. We are creatures of habit. We lead lives fueled by both healthy and unhealthy habits that dictate our way of being in the world. Healthy habits may include practices such as a regular exercise routine, consistent sleep schedule, and healthy diet. Unhealthy habits, on the other hand, may include practices such as excessive drinking, recreational drugs, irregular sleep, overeating, smoking, and so on.

Consider that habits are almost always formed through the relationship between the conscious and unconscious mind. An initial decision is made in the conscious mind, and very quickly, the unconscious mind works to fulfill the conscious mind's request. The more consistently we perform a desired task or action, the greater chance it has of being stored in our memory bank and becoming a habit. If the new habit is associated with pleasure and play in some way, the greater the chances this particular habit will become automatic and a regular occurrence in our lives.

To illustrate this further, let's explore the typical profile of a habitual smoker. Consider someone who's addicted to the pattern of smoking. At one point in the past, the smoker made a conscious decision to begin smoking. Perhaps her conscious decision was inspired by friends who smoked. It appeared to be a pleasurable and socially fun way to connect. Or, perhaps the decision was influenced by the calming effect cigarettes can have on a person. Whatever the influence, the smoker made a choice. As soon as the choice to smoke was made, the unconscious mind quickly accepted the decision and most likely associated the practice with some form of pleasure, whether social connection or relief from stress. Through repetition and consistency, the practice of smoking became automatic.

In addition, the general habit of smoking is a very physical practice. Notice that smoking is essentially a form of breathing, and it directly engages the physical body. As one breathes the smoke in and out, the breath expands and has a calming effect on the entire nervous system. Remember that the unconscious mind runs the body and essentially is the physical body. In a habitual pattern, such as smoking, the unconscious mind is directly affected and influenced by this repetitive practice. Furthermore, the smoker has likely associated the practice of smoking with certain feelings of relaxation, creativity, peace, and clarity. It's obvious that a habit such as smoking can easily become integrated and trigger all the associated attributes with the unconscious mind.

To change an unhealthy habit to a healthier habit, one must reengage her conscious mind and work directly with her understanding of the relationship between the conscious mind and unconscious mind. Knowing that the unconscious mind is highly influenced by pleasure and play, much like a child, and that it hosts all our emotions and feelings, it becomes crucial that whatever the new pattern is—in replacement of the old one—these mentioned attributes of the unconscious mind must be triggered.

For example, instead of smoking, a new repetitive habit might become chewing gum when the urge to smoke hits, or taking a pleasurable walk instead of a smoke break, or phoning a friend and having a pleasurable conversation instead of using that time to smoke. Whatever the new pattern becomes, it must touch on all the attributes of the unconscious mind in a favorable and conscious way. Serious focus, resonate feeling, repetition, and mindfulness must be employed to change the pattern. With consistent effort, along with engaging all the unconscious mind attributes, you can replace an old pattern with a new pattern within thirty days.

The Habit Formula

Therefore, the formula for mindfully changing, creating, or maintaining healthy habits in your life must touch on the following conscious and unconscious attributes to be successful:

1. **Conscious decision.** The conscious mind must recognize what it is you truly want and then make a clear and committed decision. The decision must be a full, 100 percent commitment to implement the new pattern.

2. **Feeling of pleasure.** The pattern you want to implement must be pleasurable and appealing to you on all levels. You must engage your feeling center and senses. You must get excited within yourself about what you're creating. Feelings of excitement, joy, fun, enthusiasm, and love will have profound effects.

3. **Literal repetition and reminders.** You must literally repeat over and over again what it is that you desire. You must do this mentally and physically. You have to really, really want the new pattern to happen. With any internal resistance, you won't get the results you desire.

4. **Physical component.** The unconscious mind is our physical body. The more you engage and incorporate a physical aspect to your desired pattern, the more likely you'll create it. For example, jumping up and down while shouting at the top of your lungs, "I want to feel good," will be more likely to bring you a positive energy pattern than simply thinking the statement in your mind. The physical action component will produce real results. Feel it, experience it, be it! Create a physical action component to the habits you want to create.

5. **Patience.** Be kind to yourself. Forming new habits and replacing old ones can take a bit of time. You now know the steps involved in the process. You understand the conscious and unconscious mind attributes. Have some patience and make the process enjoyable. With commitment and focus, along with a little patience, you'll eventually see results. Remember, a habit can't be forced, or the unconscious mind will deem it unenjoyable

and won't integrate the new behavior. So, get excited and find the fun in this creative process.

CHAPTER 26

CREATING WITH THE UNCONSCIOUS MIND

Whatever man feels deeply or images clearly, is impressed upon the unconscious mind, and carried out in minutest detail.
—Florence Scovel Shinn

The unconscious mind is a powerful part of who we are. As you are discovering through Principle 4: Live Mind-Fully Aware, the unconscious mind plays host to many of the foundational patterns, beliefs, and programs running under the surface in our everyday lives. As you become mindfully attuned to your unconscious mind and learn how to consciously work with it, you can create a fulfilling life. The following practices are a few other ways you can consciously work with the unconscious mind to develop the life you imagine and desire.

The Power of Affirmations

An affirmation is a statement or proposition that is declared to be true. In the practice of mindfulness, affirmations play an integral role in shaping our present-moment reality. Knowing that our thinking, along with our feelings, has a great influence on the way our lives unfold, the practice of affirmations becomes a crucial aspect to shaping our lives into the form we desire. Every thought you think and every word you speak is essentially an affirmation. Consider the regular tapes that play over and over in your mind and the words you speak throughout the day in each conversation. Do the thoughts you think and the words you speak affirm what you intend for your life?

Consider someone who constantly thinks and shares that he has no money. His regular affirmations may include these inner thoughts or spoken dialogue: "I can't afford that," or, "I'm not good with money," or, "I'm never going to be able to get out of debt." Not only does he regularly think and say these types of phrases out loud, but he's in an unconscious, habitual pattern that has become his accepted reality.

In a mindfulness practice, the creation and practice of affirmations becomes a very intentional undertaking. If the person who has been affirming a lack of money was to recognize this thought pattern as a negative affirmation and consciously put effort into changing it, his entire life would shift for the better. Knowing an affirmation is a statement that affirms what one desires, the person affirming a lack of money could change his thinking and dialogue to: "Unlimited amounts of money flow into my life easily and freely," or, "I make a home for millions of dollars, and millions of dollars find a home with me."

At first, an affirmation may not feel true. Consider that if you have been in an unconscious pattern of repeating certain phrases or beliefs year after year, it will take time, commitment, and extreme dedication to shift your reality. It's important to remember that not only must your intentional thinking change, but you must also feel the new affirmation on an emotional level as an absolute and resonant truth. To create a new pattern in the unconscious mind, you must engage with it physically and emotionally. One way to evoke a new pattern physically and emotionally is to get in front of a mirror, look yourself in the eyes, and speak aloud the affirmation you're intending.

Notice what comes up on all levels as you speak the affirmation into the mirror. If there is any resistance within you, you may not be in complete resonance with the new, intended affirmation. For example, if you look in the mirror and affirm to yourself, "You are already enough, and I love you," but you're met with saboteur resistance, this may indicate you have not yet arrived at a place of believing this affirmation to be fully true. Affirmations must be charged with intentional emotion and feeling to create a super-charged reaction within your physical body. Through consistent practice, repetition, and feeling, you will begin to accept the new affirmation in your unconscious mind and start to see it integrate into your life.

One word of caution regarding affirmations: Words and feelings are powerful conductors. If the affirmations you choose to express are not in alignment with what you truly desire, you will eventually end up attracting into your life what you don't want. You may already be experiencing this. Many are unaware of the words they speak out loud and the internal dialogue regularly playing in their head. Remember the woman who had to sell her pearls for food and the man who went on sick leave because of their misaligned affirmations? The unconscious mind absorbs all we think, feel, and say as literal truth. Therefore, align yourself with the thoughts and affirmations that you truly want to create in your life.

The unconscious mind is the epicenter within us that sparks creation by way of memory, emotion, symbolic interpretation, and believing at face value what we choose to consciously feed it. To become mindful is to realize that our unconscious mind is listening on every level and fulfilling whatever we think, feel, and speak—whether we're aware of it or not. It's important to practice affirming and believing only those thoughts that will support and encourage you to move toward the life you want. As Louise Hay so powerfully asks in her lecture on prosperity, "Are your thoughts building you up, or are your thoughts beating you up on a regular basis?"

Affirmations Exercise

The following exercise is an opportunity to begin consciously integrating the practice of affirmations into your life.

Step 1: Writing an Affirmation

Begin by writing down a sentence that you want to believe is true for you. Make it a statement that affirms what you want to create in your life. I recommend pushing your edge by making this a statement that may not yet be completely true in your life, but one that you would love to see manifest. As you write the affirmation, put it in the present tense. Affirm what you desire to be already true for you, even if it's not yet true. For example, "I attract only good people into my life," is a stronger affirmation choice than, "I would like to someday attract good people into my life." You must step fully into your intention as if what you're envisioning has already arrived in your life. If you have a difficult time stating the affirmation to be fully true, you can preface it with the phrase, "I want to believe that . . ." For example, "I want to believe that I attract only good people into my life." Over time, you can remove the initial preface ("I want to believe") and simply state the full affirmation to be true. You'll have to use your emotional gauge to monitor when you fully believe the affirmation to be true.

Step 2: Emotional Charge

Remember that the affirmation you choose to think and speak out loud must also be felt emotionally within you. For example, if you write down, "I am loveable," but don't currently feel this on an emotional level to be resonant and true, you won't see the results. Even if you are not yet totally convinced on an emotional level that your affirmation is true, you must find the place within yourself that can imagine and feel this to be possible. Otherwise, you're simply stating a phrase that has no emotional resonance. Expect that when you "feel into" an affirmation successfully, it will affect your heart center. You may feel a welling up of tears or perhaps a great charge of excitement or some other powerful emotion that indicates you're moving toward resonant truth.

Step 3: Speak

Speak your affirmation out loud several times a day until you see the results. You may even choose to say your affirmation out loud while looking into a mirror. Mirrors don't lie. They reflect nothing back but the non-judgmental truth. While speaking your affirmation to the mirror, if you see or feel resistance, you still have work to do to fully integrate the affirmation as a new pattern in your life. When you speak your affirmation and feel it fully in your heart to be true, you will soon see your life shift into the new way of being. Remember that an affirmation spoken without feeling is less likely to come to fruition than one spoken with conviction and intention.

Remember, the practice of affirmations is a mindfulness practice that involves the conscious thinking mind and all the attributes of your unconscious mind. Engage them all and intentionally make them work for you.

Vision Boards

Another mindfulness practice to complement and accentuate the powerful use of affirmations is vision boarding. Vision boarding is an effective method for aligning with and attracting into your life what you desire. For those who are unfamiliar, a vision board is a visual and symbolic representation of what you want to attract into your life. It works directly with your conscious and unconscious mind to intentionally create the life you're imagining.

To create a vision board, you'll need a blank sheet of paper—I prefer Bristol-board paper—along with a glue stick and a variety of magazines and newspapers. Next, cut out images that align with your vision and strategically place them on the blank canvas.

A few years ago, I created a vision board to align myself with the vision of writing this book. I spent time cutting out images and trigger words from magazines. The images and words I decided to incorporate onto my board motivated and inspired me, both mentally and emotionally, toward my dream of writing this book. As I pasted the words and images that resonated with me, I could feel my inner spirit grow more and more excited. Not only was I creating a visual representation of how it would feel to write this book, I was also impressing this dream onto my unconscious mind.

Upon completion, I strategically placed the board on my bedroom wall where I would see it every day for the following four years. Through a combination of seeing the board and feeling into it each day, my unconscious mind absorbed this vision into memory. What at first seemed like an impossible dream (to write a book) has now become a reality in the physical world.

Vision Board Exercise

In the spirit of mindfulness and understanding the power of your unconscious mind, I encourage you to create a vision board for yourself. Here are a few tips and suggestions to get you started. This is a very significant and powerful way to bring more intention and mindfulness into your life.

1. Get a blank sheet of Bristol-board paper or any blank canvas.
2. Gather a glue stick, scissors, and a stack of used magazines.
3. Spend time dreaming about what you want to create in your life. Be crystal clear with your vision because fuzzy targets don't get hit.
4. Once you have a clear vision, write your vision sentence in the present tense and state it like an affirmation. For example, "I am the owner of a beachfront home in Maui, Hawaii." The more specific and direct, the better. Give your unconscious mind clear direction. Make sure the affirmation you write resonates with you. Although there may still be some hesitation, push past the Saboteur and feel what it would be like to have your vision come true. Remember, you will see it when you believe it.
5. The next step is to cut words and images from the magazines. Choose images and words that evoke emotions within you and make you feel aligned with your ultimate vision. Try to find words that support your vision statement—words that describe how you will feel when this vision has been realized. For example, words such as "joyful," "ah!" "excited," and "inspired" are descriptive words with feeling.
6. Paste the images and words onto your canvas. Feel excitement as you see yourself stepping into this new reality.

7. Upon completion, place your vision board somewhere you will see it daily. The unconscious mind operates on patterns and will remember what you're envisioning by seeing the board on a regular basis.

8. Let go and allow the process to take place. Incorporate affirmations into your thinking and into every relevant conversation. For example, if someone asks what you've been up to, you may respond with a statement such as, "I'm on my way to moving to Maui, Hawaii," or, "I'm writing a book." A funny fact: For three years before I actually started writing this book, I told people that I was writing it. In my mind, this book was already completed. I was living with the feeling of a wish fulfilled. It was just a matter of time and alignment with my unconscious mind before the birth of my book happened in the physical world. Through the practice of vision boarding, you too can create what you've been imagining for yourself.

CHAPTER 27

A DYNAMIC RELATIONSHIP

There is a deep wisdom within our very flesh, if we can only come to our senses and feel it.
—**Elizabeth A. Behnke**

So far, we have explored many of the attributes associated with the conscious and unconscious mind. These two parts of the mind are not separate but, in fact, deeply connected to each other in a dynamic way. We see a direct and crucial relationship as the conscious and unconscious mind work in tandem. Remember, they are two of the three aspects involved in coming to a deeper understanding of mindfulness.

The conscious and unconscious mind are in constant contact with each other. The moment we think a thought or make a decision, the unconscious mind remembers the decision, stores it as memory, and starts working toward fulfilling the request of the conscious mind. When we come to realize that the dynamic relationship between the conscious and unconscious mind can assist us in aligning with specific memories, feelings, and strong visions for the life we desire, the possibilities are endless. Whenever we turn our attention toward the unconscious mind, it will communicate with us through visions, sensations, memories, and an inner-gut knowing that we often experience when we are aware and present.

Meditation Can Save You Air Miles

Over the past decade, the practice of meditation has become increasingly popular in our society. Although it dates back to the ancient Hindu traditions of Vedantism around 1500 BC, meditation has found a significant place in our modern-day culture. Many people have found great solitude and peace through this practice, and individuals may choose from varying forms of meditation including: chanting, breathing, silence, visualization, concentration, and focus.

In the Making Sense of Mindfulness framework, one form of meditation that is quite effective—and might I add, fun—involves the dynamic relationship between the conscious and unconscious mind. As previously discussed, these two parts of the mind work together. When the conscious mind deliberately connects with the unconscious mind, it's given instant access to memories, images, and wisdom. In this process, all senses awaken, and we can be transported to another time and place in our imagination.

I would like to take you on an adventure into your unconscious mind to demonstrate how this practice can have a tremendous effect on the state of your being. I invite you to read through the following instructions and take a few minutes to practice this exercise.

Mindfulness Meditation Exercise

Close your eyes and relax. Let go of all distractions and narrow your mental focus to your breath. Allow all the physical tension in your body to release on each exhale. As you relax, let your imagination take you to a place that is completely safe and relaxing. You may choose to visualize a place you have been before or make up a new place in your imagination as you go. The important thing is to simply let your imagination dream up a relaxing place.

Take a few moments in this relaxing place to explore the environment. First, what colors do you see? Pause until you become fully aware of all the colors surrounding you. What do you smell in this relaxing place? Pause until the smells become fully alive and present in your imagination. Open your ears and listen to the different sounds you hear. For example, if your relaxing place is outside, you may hear a gentle breeze blowing or waves crashing on a beach. Pause until the sounds become fully alive and present in your imagination. Next, notice what your body feels like in this beautiful place. What emotions come up within you as you relax? Pause until the feelings become fully alive and present in your imagination.

Finally, I invite you to touch something in this relaxing place to know that you are really there. Notice the texture of whatever you are touching. Pause until it becomes fully alive and present in your imagination. Let everything come so alive that you can almost taste it. Then, spend some time simply enjoying this beautiful, relaxing place you have created and arrived in. (Now that you have read through the instructions to this meditation, go ahead and try it out in your own time.)

If you actually engaged with this mediation, you may notice a shift in the way you feel, compared to how you felt before you traveled to your relaxing place. According to your unconscious mind, you literally visited this peaceful place because you utilized your senses and emotions. Depending on whether you allowed yourself to engage with this exercise, you may have felt as if you were actually there.

Remember that the unconscious mind takes everything literally. It doesn't know the difference between linear and non-linear time. It has the ability to time travel into the past or the future through the imagination. Furthermore, your unconscious mind plays host to all your senses. The moment you closed your eyes, imagined, and evoked memory, your unconscious mind assumed the memory you were experiencing was a present-moment truth.

Based on this premise, I enjoy daily trips to Maui, even though I presently live in Winnipeg. Every morning when I wake up, I take a trip in my unconscious mind to Kaanapali Beach. I see and hear the waves crashing on the shore; I feel my toes digging into the soft sand; I feel the rising sun warm my skin; I feel a gentle breeze blowing on my face; I hear the sound of birds in flight; and I allow my body-mind to relax and enjoy the magic of this place. Before too long, I'm literally in Maui and feel a calm, peaceful feeling flow throughout my whole body. When I open my eyes, I feel as if I have been on vacation and can move into the day ahead with a new state of being. The best part is that I have saved thousands of dollars and Air Mile points by simply engaging with this beautiful meditation practice each morning. Without having to fly to Maui, I can go there whenever I choose.

Remember, your unconscious mind runs your physical body. If you have been dreaming thoughts and meditating on images of fear, panic, worry, and doubt, expect your physical body to tighten up and cause you anxiety and stress. If you regularly choose to visit places of peace and relaxation in your meditations, you will experience continuous feelings of joy, peace, and harmony within the cells of your body. Your state of being will change, and you may find the stress you once had dissolving.

I encourage you to carve out a few minutes each day to travel to your destination of choice in your unconscious mind. Even if you feel stuck, and the stress is piling up in your life, take a few minutes out of your day to cash in your unconscious mind Air Miles and take a trip. The results are tremendous. Your stress levels will decrease, and you'll realize that even in difficult situations, you can shift your state and reconnect to inner peace. No matter the chaos that may surround you, you have the opportunity to visit your secret garden of relaxation anytime you choose, free of charge. Close your eyes and go there now.

CHAPTER 28

THE CONSCIOUS AND UNCONSCIOUS MIND RECAP

Minds are like flowers, they open when the time is right.
—**Stephen Richards**

We have now explored two of the three aspects of Principle 4: Live Mind-Fully Aware. Before discussing the third aspect of your mind, I would like to briefly review the main attributes associated with the conscious and unconscious mind. The main attribute of the conscious mind is that of **making decisions.** Every time you make a decision, it **generates a pattern.**

The unconscious mind is a bit more complex in its functions. The main attributes of the unconscious mind are the following:

- **It holds all memory.** Like a hard drive, the unconscious mind stores all our memory.

- **It runs the body.** It ensures our body continues to function (e.g., heartbeat, breathing, digestion).
- **It is literal.** It doesn't have a filter and takes everything at face value.
- **It hosts our emotions and feelings.** It's the center for all our feelings.
- **Repetition:** one of the main ways that the unconscious mind retains memory.
- **It operates and communicates with symbols and patterns.** One of its main languages is symbolism, and it also operates through the use of patterns.
- **It is drawn to pleasure and play.** Like a young child, the unconscious mind is attracted to pleasure and playfulness.

CHAPTER 29

THE HIGHER SELF

To see a World in a Grain of Sand
And a Heaven in a Wild Flower
Hold Infinity in the palm of your hand
And Eternity in an hour
—**William Blake**

The third aspect of Principle 4 can be a difficult one to grasp. It's not something tangible that we can see with our eyes or touch with our hands. As soon as one tries to define and name this third aspect, its essence is lost. It takes on a physical form and becomes a construct of the conscious mind. Many have tried to encapsulate what makes up this third aspect of being mindfully aware, and the only truth that has prevailed is that this third aspect is solely experiential in nature; it's experienced in our lives but cannot be tangibly defined. It is truly elusive.

Although mysterious in nature, the qualities and presence of this third aspect is everywhere and in everything. The closest name I can use to describe it, without its essence being lost, is what I'll refer to as the "higher self." Whether you choose to call it the higher self, God, Buddha, Krishna, Allah, source, spirit, energy, oneness, or divinity, it's not the name that is of significance but, more so, the essence. Understanding the qualities and characteristics of the higher self is what's important.

Many have confused religion with the higher self, suggesting that this aspect is associated with a specific religious tradition. What I'm referring to as the higher self is not a specific religion; instead, it's a reference to assist me in describing that which flows deeper than any one, human-made religion could define. If this aspect were religiously based, it would be mistaken for a conscious mind aspect and would no longer carry the essence of what I'm referring to.

Many wars and conflicts have erupted over the years between cultures and religions, defending one position or another. It seems that the collective Saboteur between these adversaries has convinced both sides that one way is right while the other is wrong. It's important to understand that with a mindfully aware perspective, no one gets to be right and no one has to be wrong. The higher self is in everyone and everything and cannot be fully grasped or defined by this temporary world.

CHAPTER 30

ATTRIBUTES OF
THE HIGHER SELF

If the doors of perception were cleansed everything would appear to man as it is, infinite.
—William Blake

Pierre Teilhard de Chardin once wrote, "We are spiritual beings having a temporary human experience." Have you ever considered that everything of this physical world is temporary? From the clothes you are wearing to the book you are reading, from the hair on your head to your existence on this planet, everything in physical form has an expiration date. So many of us live in denial, yet we too will one day perish. In Principle 4: Live Mind-Fully Aware, we come to realize we are more than our conscious mind, the aspect in which most of us operate; we also have an unconscious mind and a higher self. As we come to recognize these two other aspects, we eventually awaken and see more to life than our temporary human condition.

Although this physical body will eventually dissolve, what remains is the spirit of who we are. What is this spirit aspect, and how do we know it exists? These questions are answered by exploring the attributes of the higher self.

Years ago, one of Swami Muktananda's students asked him, "What is real?" His reply: "That which is real never changes." Consider that everything in physical form is in a constant state of change. You don't have to look far outside of yourself to realize this truth. When I look back at photos of myself from twenty years ago, I can see that the body I was in then is no longer the body I now occupy. My hair has thinned out, and I have developed a few more wrinkles on my forehead. Even on a cellular level, the cells of our body have a finite life span and will eventually replace themselves. In fact, since you picked up this book, you are no longer in the same body that sat down to read it. You have changed on many levels. According to Muktananda, all that appears in this physical world is constantly changing and, therefore, is not real. The question thus becomes, what never changes?

As you will come to see, that which never changes is the higher self aspect to who we are. It's the eternal source of oneness we are all connected to and the source that stimulates new ideas. It's the source that ensures a sunrise every morning and every evening, a sunset. It's the one source behind every breath you take, every blink of your eyes, and every heartbeat. So that you can experience and understand this infinite part of who you are, I will outline some of the main attributes associated with the higher self.

Creativity

The higher self is our creativity. It's the part responsible for the inventive thoughts and inspiring expressions we contribute to the physical world.

From every song to every innovative business idea, the higher self is the source behind it all. It's through the higher self that we receive those "aha" moments, along with original ways to problem solve and express ourselves in the physical world.

It's common to hear an artist speak about the creative process and give credit to the unseen source behind the work she has produced. For example, consider these words from famous dancer and choreographer Martha Graham:

> There is a vitality, a life force, an energy, a quickening that is translated through you into action, and because there is only one of you in all of time, this expression is unique. And if you block it, it will never exist through any other medium and it will be lost. The world will not have it. It is not your business to determine how good it is nor how valuable nor how it compares with other expressions. It is your business to keep it yours clearly and directly, to keep the channel open. You do not even have to believe in yourself or your work. You have to keep yourself open and aware to the urges that motivate you.

Many songwriters, dancers, painters, authors, creators, and even entrepreneurs speak about their creative process and attribute the success of their work to the unseen source behind it. As a songwriter myself, I can attest to an unseen, creative source that inspires the lyrics and melodies of my songs. Although I can't see this creative source, I experience it regularly when, out of thin air, an idea enters my awareness from the higher self and, before too long, takes on a physical form in a new song.

Even as I sit here on the floor of my meditation room and transcribe these words onto the page, I am in awe of how these words flow out, with no preconceived formula or intention beyond knowing that I have been inspired to write a book. I am witnessing, in this present moment, the creative power of the higher self.

The higher self is available to everyone, and you can witness it in all things. From the blooming of a flower to the changing of seasons to the different colors of a rainbow, the higher self is constantly expressing itself through creativity. Notice that all your thoughts, ideas, and imaginings originate from an unseen source. We who are mindfully aware call this source our higher self.

Connection

Have you ever been affected by a tragic news story, and without even knowing the victims, found yourself empathizing with them? On December 14, 2012, when I learned of the tragic school shootings in Newton, Connecticut, I was deeply saddened by the loss. Although I did not know any of the students who were murdered, nor their families, I felt connected to them and was moved to tears.

The same thing happened for me during the tragic events of September 11, 2001. As I watched the World Trade Center crumble to the ground, I was deeply shocked and saddened by these horrific acts of terror. Although I did not personally know the victims, my heart went out to their families. There was something inside of me that felt universally connected to these people. The feeling of oneness was bigger than my individual self. It was a collective, global feeling of connection that came over me. I had no choice but to feel the pain of this tragic event.

It's not only tragic events that remind us of our innate connection to others on our planet. Joyful moments can evoke the same realization. As I described earlier, the moment I stood before my entire elementary school and led all the students in song also inspired a feeling of connection. As I looked out over the singing crowd, I realized, in that moment, that there was truly no separation between us. All the things that appear to separate us fade away when we join in song. We are connected.

The time I engaged with the people of Kenya in an impromptu jam session in the middle of the Masai Mara marketplace was also one of those moments when I experienced how all things are connected. Although we did not speak the same language, the music brought us together and reminded us that we all share this planet together. We all breathe the same air, share the warmth of the same sun, and sleep under the same moon at night. We are a connected universe, singing to the same "unified-verse" of a song we have come to call life.

It's through the higher self that we are all connected. Unlike the concept of the Saboteur, which suggests everything is separate, the higher self deeply connects everything together. In the practice of mindfulness, it becomes extremely important to understand that every thought we think and every word we speak ripples out and affects the world around us. Even if we try to avoid it, we return to this profound truth: Through the higher self, all things are connected.

Synchronicity

Another attribute of the higher self is that of synchronicity. Have you ever had the experience of randomly thinking about somebody, and a few moments later that very person calls you? How about the time you were humming a song in your head, and it just happened to play on the radio? Although it may seem simply to be a coincidence, in mindful awareness, we come to realize these synchronized events are, in fact, an expression of our higher self in action.

A few years ago, I found myself scheduled to instruct a nine o'clock yoga class at the studio where I teach and practice. It was a Wednesday evening, and my wife, Kristen, was out of town. In my house, Kristen is definitely the master chef and ensures we eat three meals a day.

Whenever Kristen is away, I must confess that I don't eat as well and sometimes forget to even eat at all. On that particular evening, with an empty stomach and a slight feeling of dizziness, I stood at the front of the yoga class and told the students that I hadn't eaten much and would most likely refrain from walking around the room while teaching.

Immediately following the class, to my surprise, I was approached by one of the students who introduced himself as Brad. Brad explained to me that just prior to leaving for the yoga studio, he had put a pot of soup on the stove to enjoy when he got home. After hearing about my empty belly and Kristen being away, Brad invited me to come over for a bowl of soup. I have to be honest, my first reaction to Brad's invitation was fueled by my saboteur. I immediately thought of all the reasons I shouldn't go: *It's much too late to go over to a stranger's house for soup . . . What if Brad is a serial killer? . . . This just seems a bit weird . . . At half past ten, a stranger's house for a bowl of soup? . . . You better not go!*

Despite all the saboteur resistance I was experiencing, there was a silent whisper inside of me, urging me to go. I decided to pay attention to the whisper and found myself driving to Brad's house at half past ten for a bowl of soup. When I arrived, I was greeted with the smell of home-cooked soup, boiling on the stove. Brad invited me in, and we shared a meal together.

As we ate, I asked Brad questions about his life and family. When we discussed his family, Brad's eyes teared up, and he expressed to me that his wife, Carolyn, had passed away a year ago and that this particular evening marked their wedding anniversary. He explained that Carolyn always loved to feed people, and when he heard my story of not eating much that day, he was compelled to invite me over for a bowl of soup to commemorate his anniversary and honor the kindness of his wife. Upon hearing this, I too felt my eyes get watery and my throat well up. It was a beautiful, sacred moment that could not possibly have been planned.

As we were discussing Carolyne and the wonderful woman that she was, the lights in the kitchen intermittently flickered, as if an aspect of her spirit was acknowledging our tribute to her. While the lights flickered, I felt a chill run down my spine and an extremely deep feeling of gratitude and love come over me. For if I hadn't listened to that inner whisper urging me to go to Brad's house—and had instead become a victim of my saboteur—I would have missed out on a divinely synchronized event, one most definitely inspired by the higher self. When we learn how to pay attention to our higher self, we find ourselves experiencing tiny miracles every day. We see that synchronicity is a common bond we all share.

The higher self is what moves the checker pieces of our lives into the proper order so that everything unfolds exactly as it should, delivering us exactly what we need in each moment. It is this part of our mind in mindful awareness that causes apparent miracles to take place. Along with being creative in nature and connected to everything, the higher self is instrumental in aligning us with the perfect time and the perfect place, always and in all ways.

The following sections are an excerpt from my journal that further illustrates the magic that happens when connected to the higher self aspect of who we are.

The Rainbow Miracle

As I sit here on the floor, kneeling down and writing these words, I am overwhelmed and overjoyed by the perfection of life. I am currently on a three-week vacation and writing trip in Maui. I came here to continue working on the book and to pay tribute to Dr. Wayne Dyer, who resided here on this island before his death. I wanted to be in Maui to finish this book, knowing that this is a place where Wayne wrote many of the books that inspire me. As I scribble down the words on this page regarding our higher self, I am overlooking Kaanapali Beach, the same beach where Wayne walked and swam daily. I can feel his spirit soaring in the air here, and I see his spirit and energy present in everything.

This morning, I went for a drive to one of my favorite locations in Maui, the Nakalele Blowhole. Due to a unique formation along the edge of the shore, this blowhole was formed over time as the sea caves grew landward and upward into a vertical shaft, exposing themselves to the surface of the land. As one stands admiring this natural blowhole, waves of water from the ocean crash at the shore and shoot straight up from underneath the shore's surface. Much like a whale's spout, bursts of water shoot up into the air, reaching over one hundred feet high at times.

As I sat by the blowhole this morning, I went into a short meditation and connected with Wayne Dyer. I asked him to give me a sign that he was still present and alive in spirit. As I opened my eyes, a huge burst of water shot up through the blowhole and left a mist that formed a perfect rainbow in front of me. Stretching at least twenty feet wide and one hundred feet tall, this rainbow was a sure sign that Wayne was present. Not only did the rainbow appear once, but it reappeared for the following fifteen minutes each time a burst of water shot up from the blowhole.

I sat on the rocks in absolute awe and joy, knowing this was all happening perfectly on time. To a passerby, this may have simply been a neat-looking rainbow, but to me, this was a confirmation from my higher self that Wayne was present in spirit, and that we truly are all connected by means of this incredible source known as the higher self.

A Few Days Later
A few days passed after the miraculous rainbow at Nakalele Blowhole. I received a text message from one of my best friends in Winnipeg, informing me of a conference taking place with well-known spiritual author Deepak Chopra. I took this message as a sign from my higher

self that I should explore the possibility of attending this event. As it turned out, the event was taking place five minutes from where I had been staying in Maui. I decided to drive to the conference to see if I could attend the event. Upon arriving, the organizer informed me that the event had been sold out for months. I told the event organizer that if there were any last-minute cancellations or openings, I would be interested.

I further explained to her that I was in Maui working on a book and paying my respects to Wayne Dyer, who happened to be a close friend of Deepak Chopra. The organizer took my contact information and told me she would be in touch if anything became available. A bit discouraged, I wandered back toward my hotel. Within ten minutes of leaving the conference, I received a message from the organizer informing me she felt I needed to be there and that she could offer me a complimentary guest pass to attend the event—free of charge. I returned to the conference site and learned that this particular conference was originally scheduled to be co-facilitated by Deepak Chopra and Wayne Dyer. Unfortunately, because of Wayne's passing, the event would be hosted exclusively by Deepak. Upon hearing this, I was instantly overtaken with tears, and another chill ran down my spine.

In that moment, I realized this was yet another message from my higher self, which is connected to everything. I had an immediate, inner knowing that these events had been divinely orchestrated and that Wayne was literally putting me on his "guest list" for the event. I took this as another sign of his spirit, alive and responsive there. Although Wayne is no longer here in a physical body, it became quite obvious as the conference unfolded that Wayne's spirit was definitely present and alive. This was yet another sign from my higher self that I was supposed to receive this gift of synchronicity.

I share these stories of synchronicity in my own life because they demonstrate how our higher self operates. When we mindfully pay attention and connect to all three aspects of ourselves in the Live Mind-Fully Aware Principle, we find that all we need and ask for is delivered to us in a synchronistic way; it's our higher self in action.

Oneness

I have always been fascinated by the subtle yet extreme difference between the words, "nowhere" and "now here." Although both contain the same letters and are spelled with the same letter configuration, they have dissimilar meanings. A simple space between the words "now" and "here" changes the entire meaning.

Consider where you came from. Consider where everything in this physical world originated. It all began from the place we can refer to as "nowhere." This nowhere place is impossible to define, control, or tangibly grasp. What we do know, however, is that this place of nowhere cannot be separated into pieces. It's not directly seen in the physical world. From what we know, the place of nowhere is a place of infinite potentiality. From this place of infinite possibility, we are suddenly born and take on a physical form in the world. We are born into a state we refer to as "now here." In this state of "now here," we spend a finite amount of time exploring and expressing ourselves in the physical world, and then we take a return trip back to our place of origin, nowhere.

Through this cycle of nowhere to now here and then back to nowhere, it seems we are destined to constantly return to the place of nowhere. In fact, it is in this state of nowhere that we find unlimited creative potential and inseparable, complete oneness. The place of nowhere is the one constant that appears to be guaranteed. It never changes, and it's what we all have in common.

T. S. Eliot writes, "We shall not cease from exploration, and the end of all our exploring will be to arrive where we started and know the place for the first time." In essence, our higher self is eternally rooted in the constant oneness that appears to be found in the place of nowhere.

It's the one guarantee that is certain throughout our physical expression on the planet: We have been born into the physical world, and at some point we will cease to be "now here" and return to the source from which we came, "nowhere."

To the Saboteur, which lives in our conscious mind, the thought of making a return trip to the place from which we originated (nowhere) is a terrifying one. As we explored earlier in Principle 2, the Saboteur operates from a place of separation and fear. It's conditioned to believe that everything is separate and that the surrender of our physical form and the acquisitions we have gained in the "now here" should be avoided at all costs. It does not understand that absolute peace is found in the oneness which exists beyond the physical form we are temporarily experiencing.

The higher self operates from the standpoint that the infinite source from which we came (nowhere) is the ultimate constant and represents who we truly are. No separation exists in the realm of nowhere. Through an invisible, creative energy that can't be permanently separated, we are united as one. Quantum physics proves to us that "separation is simply a useful illusion." While living in this physical world, it's essential that we have a separate, physical identity so that we can authentically express ourselves and not morph into each other. For if we did not have our separate identities here on earth, we would literally be unable to distinguish ourselves from one another and would most likely be a giant blob of oneness, with no unique distinctions. The truth is that our origin, our infinite potential, and the life force that flows through us and is expressed into the temporary, physical form is rooted in one infinite source.

One of the main attributes of the higher self is that of oneness. It cannot be separated. This may explain why the higher self aspect of the Live Mind-Fully Aware Principle cannot be seen in a tangible form in the physical world. It simply cannot be separated. It lives in everyone and everything, and its presence is truly oneness, whereby under the surface of physical form, everything literally is everything.

If you take a moment right now and let yourself be still, you may get a glimpse into this life force moving through you and everything else around you. Can you sense that it is a shared life force which grows the plants and makes the hearts of every living creature beat? It's the same life force that provides the creative ideas within your imagination. Can you look up at the sky and see yourself in every shining star that glistens down on the earth? Can you see you share this life source with the ocean and all the creatures that swim in it? Can you sense the shared life source that unites you with the elderly and the dying? Can you sense your connection to the newborn baby? Can you sense the shared life source that animates the birds, the bees, the flowers, the sun, the moon, and the planets and sense they are all, at the same time, operating within you? Can you look out into the world and see every human being you encounter as a direct reflection and connection to yourself? To see the unified spirit that lives within each physical being on this planet, and to recognize that this spirit is also you is to know the higher self. It's an inseparable oneness.

Aloha

Another way to comprehend the essence of oneness is to understand the practice of Aloha. Aloha is an ancient Hawaiian practice that encapsulates the essence of what it means to live in oneness with the higher self. Translated into English, "Aloha" means "love is to be happy with." "Alo" means shared unity. "Oha" means affection, and "Ha," as described earlier, means breath and life force. Known as a state law and a common greeting in Hawaii, the deeper meaning of Aloha is a practice of seeing the divine, the higher self, within everyone you meet and everything around you. It is being a literal embodiment of oneness while living on the planet in physical form. Aloha is to share love with all that crosses your path and to see each aspect of this life as a piece of yourself.

To look out at the world and realize your inherent oneness with all you see is a sacred practice that often gets neglected. In the practice of Aloha, we are reminded that all of life is sacred and unified. It cannot be separated, although it appears to be that way in the physical form. In the practice of mindfulness, we come to realize that to love all the life that surrounds us and to be in harmony with each and every being, we must first love and accept ourselves, knowing that all is one and the same. To truly begin understanding the higher self aspect of who we are requires us to open our minds and believe that all is truly one. We are united by the great spirit, which lives in all of us.

The powerful words of St. Francis of Assisi remind us, "In dying we are born to eternal life." I have always been fascinated by the concept and practice of "dying while you are alive." Have you ever considered that all the concrete and permanent structures that currently surround us in this physical world are merely temporary illusions that will eventually return to the state of no-thing from which they came? If you can comprehend and accept that every "thing" in this physical world is not permanent, you're on your way to discovering what it means to be born into eternal life, and to live from the place of oneness while you are consciously here on the planet.

You are no longer attached to all the petty details that have consumed your attention. Instead, you find yourself surrendering to the shared oneness flowing beneath the surface in all of life. In a mindfulness practice, you are invited to step outside of your physical attachments and ponder the possibility that you are one with all and all is one with you, for this is a major attribute of understanding your higher self.

Gratitude

The higher self is most often accessed by moving into a state of gratitude. To truly feel a sense of gratitude deep within every part of you is to consciously awaken to your higher self. Have you ever noticed that it's impossible to be angry and upset when you are fully embracing a state of genuine gratitude? It's impossible to feel separate and isolated when you are experiencing gratitude.

Gratitude reminds us that we are all one. It helps us to come into deep appreciation of and awareness that through our inherent oneness, we've been granted all we have asked for, and everything is unfolding exactly as it should, in the perfect time and place. Gratitude reawakens us to the higher self and reminds us, even in the challenging moments, that life is more than the temporary illusions we are currently facing.

I recommend incorporating a gratitude practice into your daily life. Whether it be writing in a gratitude journal, making a daily list of ten things you are grateful for, or sending a personal card of thanks to someone who has blessed your life, a regular practice of gratitude will ensure that you are operating in union with the higher self.

Generosity

One of the most important attributes of the higher self is that it will always work toward giving you what you ask for. Whether you are conscious of it or not, the higher self is in a constant state of creativity, love, and generosity. Consider that all which has shown up in your life, both good and bad, was created and delivered to you by the highest part of yourself. Whether it was attracting the ideal mate at the right time or delivering you the career you currently have, the higher self is in a constant state of giving and creating. It does not play favorites, and it works with you to create the life you have been dreaming about.

If you recall, the thoughts you think about on a regular basis will greatly determine what shows up in your life. The higher self will always give you the closest equivalent to what you are asking for, based on where you are in your life and what is actually needed. For example, if you desire to be a multi-millionaire but are not in the current head space to attract that kind of wealth, you may just see a commercial on TV promoting the million dollars you asked for. If your thinking has been misaligned in some way, you will begin to see these thoughts delivered into your life by your higher self. You are always delivered that which you have been focusing your attention on, so focus on what you want to create. What is important to understand is that the higher self will always deliver what you ask for. In fact, it wants to play an instrumental role in fulfilling your life's purpose on this planet.

CHAPTER 31

THE MIND-FULLY
AWARE FORMULA

Perhaps we should love ourselves so fiercely that when others see us they know exactly how it should be done.
—Rudy Francisco

N ow that we have taken an extensive look at the attributes comprising the three aspects of your mind in the Live Mind-Fully Aware Principle, I will explain how these three parts communicate with each other. I will also offer practical steps for applying this mindfulness principle to your everyday life. I call these steps of practical application the Mind-Fully Aware Formula.

As we discovered, the conscious mind, which is responsible for making decisions, has a direct relationship with the unconscious mind. If you recall, the unconscious mind is the part that holds all memory, runs the body, plays host to our emotions and feelings, runs all the patterns in our lives, and takes everything literally, at face value. These two aspects, the conscious mind and the unconscious mind, communicate with each other back and forth on a regular basis. When we think a thought in the conscious mind, it's remembered in the unconscious mind and body. The opposite is also true in that when we focus our conscious mind's attention on the unconscious-body mind, we are able to recall certain memories, become aware of patterns running in our lives, and feel our feelings and emotions.

This leaves us with the third aspect to who we are, the higher self, which plays host to all our creativity, intuition, innovation, wisdom, and connection to oneness. How do we make conscious contact with the higher self? The answer is that the higher self does not communicate directly with the conscious mind. It does not give the conscious mind direct access to the creative wisdom available to us. This is because as human beings in this temporary physical world, we are given free will to make the choices and decisions we choose to make with our conscious mind. The higher self does not interfere with our free will to make decisions.

To access the creative wisdom of our higher self, we must experience it through the unconscious-body mind. For our deepest wisdom and creativity of the higher self is accessed through the channel of the unconscious mind. This explains why our intuition is always based in various aspects of our body, including the heart and the gut center. When we experience our intuition, it's experienced in our physical body as sensation or a silent inner-knowing. In essence, our intuition is the language in which our higher self consciously communicates with us.

For, to truly work with our creativity and higher self energy, we must learn to focus on our physical body and intuition. The higher self gives the conscious mind, our decision-making center, free will to decide what we want for ourselves. It respects our decision making so much as not to interfere; instead, it honors the decisions our conscious mind makes and works toward granting us the fulfillment of each desire and wish we dream for ourselves.

Therefore, to truly understand this formula, we must come to see that our conscious mind is the decision-making control center, whereby that which we choose to think about and create stems from our thinking. The unconscious mind plays the role of remembering what our conscious mind desires and then serves these desires by working with the higher self. The unconscious mind also serves as a channel through which our higher self can communicate with our conscious mind (known as intuition). Finally, the higher self part of us, which is connected to everything and holds all creativity in eternity, collaborates with the unconscious mind to carry out that which we desire and yearn for in our lives. This completes a perfect formula by which we can explain how all becomes born into our world.

The Mind-Fully Aware Formula in Action

So that you may fully understand the Mind-Fully Aware Formula and put it into action, I will give you two examples of how this formula can operate in your daily life.

Example 1: I'm So Tired

Suppose you wake up in the morning, and before you even roll out of bed, you find yourself thinking in your conscious mind, "I am *so* tired." As you think this thought, your conscious mind makes the decision that you did not get enough sleep the night before and that you are now going to feel tired. As you place your feet on the floor and walk toward the bathroom to brush your teeth, your unconscious mind begins to feel the desire of the conscious mind. "I am *so* tired," it insists, initiating a yawn in your body, as if to suggest that you really are tired. Before you even leave for work, you find yourself wanting to fall back asleep, and you experience an overwhelming feeling of exhaustion come over your entire body.

Does this sound familiar? From what has taken place already, it appears obvious that your conscious and unconscious minds have started working together to ensure that you will be tired as you go through your day. As you drive to work, your higher self connects with your unconscious mind's pattern of being tired and accepts it as true.

The next thing you know, you turn on the radio, and the first commercial you hear is an advertisement for a mattress company, alluding to sleep. Although you may simply take it as coincidence, your higher self has begun to magnify your desire to be tired and has offered the indicator that your wish is being fulfilled.

As you arrive at work, the higher self becomes so committed to fulfilling your decision to be tired that it delivers tired coworkers for you to visit with. As you enter the office, the first person you meet exclaims how tired she is, and before too long, you find yourself surrounded by a group of staff members and customers who all appear to share the common bond of being tired. These are all supposed gifts from your creative higher self. The day continues, and you receive ample opportunities to carry out your conscious mind's request to be tired. This decision to be tired may eventually become a regular pattern in your life and an accepted reality for the average "sleepy Joe," who is unaware of the Mind-Fully Aware Formula.

The one who understands the Mind-Fully Aware Formula, however, will not be manipulated by such a pattern. Although at first it may seem like an exaggeration, the one who truly wants to feel rested on a consistent basis in his life will open his eyes in the morning and know that the initial thoughts he thinks in his conscious mind will play a major role in determining the outcome for his day.

While waking up in the morning, a practitioner of the Mind-Fully Aware Formula will affirm to himself, "I am rested and ready for a great day ahead." Even if all the circumstances point to a different reality, the mindfulness practitioner will think and feel within himself that he is rested, until this desire truly becomes a reality. As you can imagine, the conscious decision to be awake will directly affect the unconscious mind's memory pattern, and the unconscious mind will adopt the feeling of being rested. Before too long, the higher self will make this desire a reality and provide all the opportunities for this practitioner to carry out his day in a well-rested state, full of life.

Note that when you try to change a pattern that has operated in your life for an extended period of time, you may at first feel resistance and possibly hear the Saboteur discouraging you from making changes. Depending on how long the undesired pattern has been in operation, the length of time it will take to implement what you desire will vary.

As suggested earlier, to truly implement a new, desired pattern can take up to thirty days of consistent effort, focus, and repetition. I encourage you to stick with the new patterns and convince yourself on all levels—mentally, physically, and emotionally—that what you want for yourself is truly possible. As soon as you believe it, feel it, and act as if it's true, the desired outcome will set into motion and arrive at the perfect time and in the perfect way.

Example 2: Learning to Love Yourself

In my younger years, I was notorious for attracting romantic relationships into my life that would always end in heart break. It was almost a given that no matter who I dated, they would cheat on me. At the time, I consistently found myself broken hearted, convinced I would never find a relationship that truly supported me. I believed that there was no such thing as an honest partner, and no matter who I chose to be with, the fear of being cheated on eventually became inevitable.

This pattern of being cheated on and lied to lasted for quite some time, until I was fortunate enough to stumble across an incredible life coach who assisted me in dissolving this painful pattern in my life. Upon beginning our work together, my coach challenged me to end the current relationship I was in with a partner who had cheated on me three times in a row. I was further challenged to take at least one year off dating and focus exclusively on learning how to love myself better.

Although this was one of the most difficult and scary things I had ever been challenged to do, I confronted my girlfriend. I told her I wanted out of the relationship and requested that she never contact me again. I was met with resistance and anger from my ex-girlfriend, along with internal saboteur thoughts telling me I was making a terrible decision. I also recall fearing that I would never find someone to share my life with. Although there was extreme resistance within me to make this change, this challenge truly became the beginning of my healing journey and discovery of what it means to apply the Mind-Fully Aware Formula to my life.

As time went by, I found myself learning new ways to truly love myself. One of these ways was revealed to me almost immediately. After the break-up, I stopped receiving daily love texts from her, and although this may seem like a minor issue, for me at the time, this added to the heartache I was already experiencing. I brought this concern up with my life coach and explained how much I was missing contact with my ex-girlfriend.

My coach challenged me to download an iPhone app that automatically texts preprogrammed messages at a pre-set time to my phone. I took this challenge and began to preprogram love texts to myself. Each day from then on began with an automated text message from myself: "I love you, Keith. You are so beautiful." These positive messages would appear on my phone throughout the day to remind me of what I wanted to believe about myself. As time went by, I found myself unconsciously seeing these positive text messages and noticed they had become new patterns and beliefs in my life.

To this day, I honor the practice of text messaging myself with positive reminders: "Remember to eat"; "You are perfectly on time"; "Trust your heart"; and "You are already enough." As I consciously remind myself, each day, of these messages, my unconscious mind slowly accepts and integrates them as truth. What results is a new way of being in the world.

Aside from this practice of texting myself, I have also developed a regular practice of daily mirror work, which involves speaking loving and kind messages to myself in front of the mirror. I also take time each day to meditate and reflect on my true feelings. To speak loving and kind messages to myself, accompanied by intentional feelings, has become a powerful way to transform my self-doubt into self-love.

These powerful practices have made me aware that the thoughts I think, the words I speak, and the actions I take on a daily basis will affect my overall state of being. It became apparent that the old beliefs which had been running in my unconscious mind's memory bank were simply programmed patterns that had been affecting all my romantic relationships, not to mention many other areas of my life. Because of these old beliefs, the higher self was delivering a string of cheating women who were successfully fulfilling this unconscious pattern I had attracted into my life.

As I became aware of these toxic patterns, I also became very curious as to where these distorted beliefs about my self-worth had originated. I spent a great deal of time focusing my attention on my unconscious mind's intuitive wisdom to find out when and where it was that I first made the decision I was not good enough. I quieted my mind and thought back to the first memory of feeling inadequate.

As I let my mind relax, I landed upon an early memory in my consciousness of where I first felt rejected. The memory took me all the way back to seventh grade. At that time, I had a dream of becoming an actor. I was fascinated with the performing arts. I learned that the local theater company was holding auditions for an upcoming production of Tennessee William's *Cat on a Hot Tin Roof*. I immediately signed up for an audition.

When the audition day arrived, my mother drove me to the theater, along with my brother, who had been home sick from school. When we arrived at the theater, we were instructed to take a seat in the waiting room. A few moments later, the artistic director of the theater company came into the room and introduced himself. Upon taking one quick look at my brother, the director decided he would be ideal for the part they were casting and hired him to be in the play. To my disappointment, my brother was granted the role I had so desperately wanted, and without truly realizing it at the time, I made the decision that I was not good enough and undeserving of success.

As time progressed, I struggled with self-esteem issues and eventually ended up in a string of dysfunctional relationships with women who were dishonest and cheated on me. Until I took the time to listen to my unconscious mind's memory pattern, I was unable to see the correlation between the memory of being rejected at that audition and the current pattern playing out in my relationships. As I now reflect on what took place in my life during those particular memories, I no longer feel resentment, hurt, and anger.

I have come to see that all the characters in my life, including my brother, the artistic director, my life coach, and the cheating women, have played a significant part in assisting me with learning how to love myself. Although none of these people realized they were playing a particular role in my life, I look back now from a mindfully aware perspective and feel nothing but gratitude for everything that took place. These people and events led me to update my patterns and recognize that I had to change my beliefs to see the changes I wanted in the world around me.

It has been over four years since I broke up with my ex-girlfriend. By deliberately applying the Mind-Fully Aware Formula and changing my thoughts, feelings, and beliefs, I have completely transformed my life and self-esteem. Just this past summer, I married the woman of my dreams, and I find myself in a truly beautiful relationship, not only with my wife but also with myself. The love we share is a reflection of the self-love we both have cultivated within ourselves.

I believe that when one mindfully chooses to become aware of the patterns in his life and consciously chooses to live in alignment with his true, ideal vision for himself, he will meet with miraculous results from the higher self. To experience this alignment, we must make a conscious commitment to a mindfully aware lifestyle. The conscious mind, the unconscious mind, and the higher self must work in tandem in order for life to truly become a place of intentional co-creation. Such was the gift I was humbly granted through these powerful teachers in my life. I learned how to truly love all parts of myself, independent of approval and love from others.

CHAPTER 32

THE MIND/BODY RELATIONSHIP

The heart has its reasons which reason knows nothing of.
—**Blaise Pascal**

To truly benefit from Principle 4 in the Making Sense of Mindfulness framework, one must consistently practice living mindfully aware in daily life. One way to effectively practice this principle is to consider the relationship between your thinking mind and your physical body. When we get the mind (conscious) and the body (unconscious) in rapport with each other, the higher self can flow in and create ideal conditions in our lives. As I mentioned earlier, the mind and body are very much like two partners in a relationship. When working together in harmony, we experience bliss; when they are in a state of disagreement, we experience hardship.

Have you ever noticed that in the relationship between your mind and body, when things are out of sync, it's most often because one partner tends to be the over-talker while the other partner tends to be the over-listener? It's very common for us to experience our mind in the relationship as the over-talker. The mind uses thoughts and ideas to communicate with the body, and when it over talks, the body can become stressed and anxious.

Consider times when your mind worried over scenarios that had yet to happen. In these moments, your mind was controlling the conversation with your body, over talking its way into false evidence appearing real (FEAR). As a result, your body became stressed, which may have played out in a variety of ways, including anxiety in the chest, sweating profusely, butterflies in the stomach, losing sleep, and so on.

As most of us have experienced, our mind tends to be the dominate personality in the relationship. As a result, the body often becomes the listener, taking instructions from the dominant mind. As we discussed in the Live Mind-Fully Aware Principle, the body/unconscious mind holds all memory and plays host to our intuition and creative higher self. In the rare moments that the physical body gets to speak in its relationship with the mind, we often experience the language of the body as intuition and/or physical sensation. Do you remember a time you knew what to do, intuitively, without overthinking it? Have gut feelings ever led you to the actual truth? In those moments, your body was leading the conversation in relationship to your mind.

In every one of us, we hold both masculine and feminine energy and have elements of both within ourselves. In our dynamic mind/body relationship, the mind tends to represent the male energy within us. This masculine energy enjoys action and activity; it's task-oriented and likes to problem solve and figure things out efficiently. It has an incredible ability to analyze situations, and it functions best when it has been given a specific task to focus on.

In contrast, the physical body tends to represent feminine energy. In general, feminine energy is intuitive, reflective, introspective, insightful, emotional, and driven by sensitivity and feelings. Feminine energy has an innate ability to simply know what is best through its direct connection to intuition, also referred to as the higher self. It has often been said that the body, much like our mothers, always knows best. It relies heavily on its sensations and feelings to communicate inspiration to us. It has an innate ability to perceive and psychically connect to the energies around us.

A few other distinctions between the mind and body are worth noting. The mind tends to operate in the world of information (in-form) and knowledge. It collects facts, dates, formulas, equations, and instruction manuals, which all originate in the temporary, physical world. The body, on the other hand, tends to operate in the world of inspiration (in-spirit) and is connected to the world of infinite spirit, which is not seen but felt and experienced—if we pay attention. Although not seen directly, the body experiences regular inspiration through deep insights, inner truths, feelings, profound wisdom, and intuitions.

Neither aspect of the mind or the body (male or female) is right or wrong, better or worse. They both have an important role to play. If we rely too heavily on the masculine information of the mind, we will find ourselves disconnected from our spirit. On the other hand, if we rely too heavily on the feminine inspiration of the body, we will find ourselves disconnected from the physical world and unable to function in our everyday lives. To achieve inner peace and alignment, both the mind and body must work together and function in tandem, offering their individual gifts and cultivating a balanced, healthy relationship. Much like any relationship, each partner brings important elements to the table that are needed to grow and function.

As I already mentioned, in the relationship between the mind and body, it's common for the mind to dominate the body and override the body's inherent wisdom. The mind chatters and natters away as we move through our day, spilling out facts, thoughts, ideas, and suggestions on how best to move forward. When the mind dominates the body's wisdom, we often find ourselves rushing, trying to appease the demands of our mind. We can easily find ourselves feeling out of balance.

In extreme cases of an overpowering mind, we may even forget to take care of ourselves in the most basic ways. When we are overly stressed by a dominating mind, we may forget to eat and nourish our bodies. We may also deny ourselves adequate time to breathe, relax, restore, and connect to our inner selves. When the mind is exclusively running our lives, we cut off the connection to our physical body's wisdom and deny it a chance to be in relationship with the mind.

When the mind denies the body a chance to speak and be heard, the body may even scream back at the mind with symptoms, such as aches, pains, and, in extreme cases, disease. When the mind refuses to listen to the body, the body has no choice but to take desperate measures to regain respect and force the mind to pay attention. Consider that everything we experience in our physical bodies, including yawning, stiffness, aches, diseases such as cancer, and so on are all messages from the body in an attempt to be heard.

Whether you're currently experiencing an imbalance between the mind and the body or have already found a healthy balance and want to maintain it, we must come to understand that true balance requires both partners in the relationship to be respectful and attentively loving. How do we successfully attain this balance?

In the common case of an over-dominating mind, we must teach the mind simply to listen. Instead of rambling on with all of its information and analytical jumble, which, in extreme cases, disconnects us from our unconscious mind and higher self, we must invite the mind to take on the task of listening to the body and its intuition. If we can convince our mind that this task will be a beneficial practice, we will find balance in our mind/body relationship. The question then becomes, how can the mind learn to listen to the body?

To truly honor and listen to the body's intuitive wisdom, we must slow down physically and mentally. We must create space and be still. For a busy mind, this request to slow down will most likely bring up the Saboteurs of resistance and hesitation. The mind must understand that to truly find inner peace, wisdom, and clarity, it must slow down and be still. It is in the stillness and the practice of focusing our mind's attention toward our intuition that we cultivate balance. When the mind learns how to listen to the body's wisdom and honors the requests and suggestions from the body, we experience balance and fulfillment. Much like a partner who honors the request of his significant other, the mind and body must learn to work together to truly understand each other. The entryway to this practice involves sacred listening.

This relationship between the mind and the body is profound. It is truly the number one relationship that must be cultivated within ourselves to experience healthy relationships in the world. An unbalanced mind/body relationship will not only cause suffering within ourselves, but also disharmony to those around us. We must learn how to listen and respect our inner selves so we can do the same with others. We must learn to honor and understand each partner and become aware of what each brings to the relationship to strengthen it.

Learning to Listen

The following is an excerpt from a journal entry I wrote regarding the relationship between my mind and body. It's an example of why it's important to cultivate a healthy mind that listens attentively to the body's wisdom:

I recently sat down to have dinner with my wife after a busy day at work. As I sat down at the dinner table, my stomach was grumbling, and my mind was sorting out all the unfinished tasks on my to-do list. Although I appeared present, in my mind, I was still sitting at my desk doing paperwork. I immediately began eating the delicious food my wife had prepared, and within less than a minute, I was already halfway through my meal.

Upon noticing this, my wife suggested that I slow down and enjoy the meal. As soon as she spoke, I immediately felt myself becoming agitated. I hadn't eaten since noon, and coming off a busy day at work, I was not feeling up for suggestions on how to eat my meal. I took a few deep breaths and realized my wife was right. I was not paying attention in the moment. I was not tasting the delicious food and savoring each bite.

Such is the way for many of us as we rush our way through the world and rarely take a moment to slow down and savor this life. I thanked my wife for reminding me of this important lesson in learning how to listen and appreciate the present moment.

Following the meal, I noticed how this pattern of mental distraction was further affecting me in many of my conversations throughout my day. While conversing with others, I found myself drifting off into mental distractions instead of being fully present in the moment. As a result, I was missing out on opportunities to meaningfully connect and truly hear what the other person was saying.

From a mindfulness perspective, it's important to practice active listening skills as they will expand our awareness of the present moment and help us come into balance. A direct outcome of active listening is the realization that everything we actually need is found in the present moment. When we slow down enough to truly listen to the present moment and our body's wisdom, all the answers we're looking for suddenly appear. Whether it's the ideal person who has the right inspiration we need to hear or simply the enjoyment of a nourishing meal that helps us relax and digest our day, it's only by way of focusing with intentional attention that we are given exactly what we need.

Exercise: How to Cultivate a Balanced Mind/Body Relationship

A practice I have found instrumental in cultivating a healthy mind/body relationship is that of learning to listen. Much like an anchoring meditation practice (as described in Principle 3: Open Your Mind), conditioning the mind to listen to the body is a very similar process, with a few added steps. I will describe the practice, and I invite you then to try it on your own:

1. Find a place to be still and silent while you practice.

2. Sit in a comfortable position and close your eyes.

3. As you close your eyes, immediately notice the state your mind is in. Is it over talking? Is it ready to focus? Is it thinking about your to-do list, etc.?

4. With your eyes closed, give your mind the task of simply listening. As mentioned earlier, the mind loves to focus on a specific task. Have your mind play the role of listener and invite it to listen to the sound of your breathing.

5. Spend a few minutes listening to your breath moving through your body. If the mind begins to wander, gently invite it back to the focus of listening to your breathing.

6. Once you feel your mind is in a state of receptivity and fully open to listening, place one of your hands on your heart center.

7. Next, shift the focus of your listening mind from your breathing to the hand placed on your heart. Listen internally to the energy of your heart. You might notice the heart beating or feel the silent but energetic feelings arising from this area of your body.

8. Once you have built rapport between your listening mind and your responsive heart, know that your heart has wisdom to share with you. Remember, your heart—and any other part of your body—tends to speak in a language of silent inner knowing, which is accompanied by a feeling of peaceful truth. Other times, the body will speak in the language of sensation, symbolism, or imagery. However the body chooses to communicate with you here, don't overthink it, as this would once again be your mind trying to dominate and control the process.

9. With your hand on your heart, have your mind ask the following question and listen *very* carefully to the immediate answer that arises within your body. Ask your heart, "What do you want for me right now?"

10. As you listen, the initial impulse that arises is usually correct. Shortly after the first thought, the mind tends to overthink it, with thoughts that may include, "Is that really my heart speaking?" or, "Are you sure?" Trust your first impulse and simply listen to your heart.

11. Upon hearing the wisdom from your heart, check in with your mind and request that your mind honor the request from your heart's wisdom. For example, if your answer to the question ("What do you want for me right now?") was, "Get more rest," ask your mind if it will honor this request and figure out a way to get a few more hours of sleep this evening. Other times, you may simply get a one-word answer, such as love. When receiving broader answers, check in with your mind to see if it understands what the heart is requesting. For example, if you get a broad answer like love, this might be an inner knowing to make amends with someone you recently had a conflict with, or it may mean simply to love yourself in this very moment. As the mind becomes more and more attuned to listening to the heart,

it will become better and better at knowing what the heart and the entire body is trying to communicate.

12. Continually practice this process as you move throughout your day. At first, this may seem challenging, especially in busy times when your mind is dominant. However, through a consistent and committed effort, you will find yourself more and more in alignment with your mind (conscious), body (unconscious), and creativity (higher self). The results are magic.

CHAPTER 33

WHO ARE YOU?

*Wisdom is knowing I am nothing, love is knowing I am everything,
and in between the two my life moves.*
—**Nisargadatta Maharaj**

I f I were to ask you, "Who are you?" how would you respond? In one
moment, you may respond with a basic answer, such as your given
name. You may say, "I am a father," or "I am a mother." You may
respond with, "I am a doctor," or "I am a teacher." The answers to this
question will vary depending on the respondent's perspective. However,
no matter the answer, one thing remains consistent in each response:
The answer will always contain the words—in some form—"I AM."

Principle 5: I AM

The words "I AM" are two of the most powerful words in our language.
These two words are regularly in our daily thoughts and conversations.
Truly, you are what you are. The words "I AM" are neutral as they do not

contain a specific perspective or judgment as to what is. They are simply a powerful statement of truth that suggests something simply exists.

In mindfulness, I AM and its variation being, YOU ARE, are two of the most important words in the practice because these neutral words represent the closest truth to describing the present moment for what it actually is. How could anyone deny, right now, as you read this book, that YOU ARE. The truth and reality we know to be 100 percent accurate in this present moment is that YOU ARE and/or I AM. We cannot deny this to be true.

It's important to know that any other aspect you observe is also what it is and is to be accepted, without judgment: this book is, the weather is, your house is, the tree is, my friends are. All of these statements are neutral and accurately true. In a practice of mindfulness, we come to realize that everything is what it is, and we abstain from judgment. As soon as we add judgment to an I AM statement, such as "I AM sad," we form a belief and/or adopt a particular perspective.

The practice of adding perspective or judgment to the neutral words I AM is not necessarily a bad practice. In fact, it would be next to impossible to avoid this tendency completely. For as we move through our day, we are constantly choosing how to look at things around us and within us. For example, right now you might be thinking, "I AM so inspired." Someone else, in this very same moment, might be thinking, "I AM so bored." Which perspective is right? Is there an accurate way to determine which statement is more truthful?

How could we possibly give one answer a higher rating? Both are simply perspectives based on the experience and, perhaps, past memory from the unconscious mind of the person noticing the neutrality in a particular way. Notice that what remains consistent is found in the neutrality of I AM. It's important to notice that how you choose to see the world within and around you is simply your personal perspective, with no right or wrong attached. It's just your current perspective on the neutrality. How you choose to look at something, however, will play a major role in determining your experience of each present moment.

I AM That I AM

I recently had an opportunity to interview one of my favorite yoga instructors, Monica Angelatos. Monica was scheduled to present at an event I was running called the "I AM Festival," a three-day festival in nature that brought together experienced presenters in many areas of wellness. The festival's main objective was to create transformational experiences and opportunities for self-reflection, community building, and inspiration.

As I sat across from Monica and conducted a pre-festival interview, I was curious to know her perspective on what I AM meant to her. How Monica responded to this question is something I will always remember, as it deepened my understanding of how powerful I AM truly is. She explained that to truly understand I AM, we must first name all the things that "I AM not." She gave various examples of all the things that "I AM not," including, I am not my possessions, I am not my reputation, I am not my job, I am not the amount of money I have in the bank, I am not the trees, I am not the birds, I am not the air, and so on.

As she listed all the various aspects she was not, Monica finally came to a conclusion: "I am nothing." She explained that if we have deemed our truth to be that we are no-thing, then, in turn, we must be everything. For when we shed our ego of separation, (the conditioned saboteur part of us which suggests that we are what we do, what we have, and what people think of us, etc.) what is left over is "no-thing," but in essence, is everything. Monica believes I AM means that we are no-thing and everything all at once in this temporary experience of consciousness.

To see another human being, a tree, a bird, an animal, a lake, leaves, and a newborn baby as all connected to the same source you originated from is to understand what it means to be connected to an awareness of

I AM. For I AM is a neutrality that connects everything together and reminds us of our essence. I AM can help us accept everything for what it truly is and what it chooses to be, knowing we are all connected by one originating source.

In essence, I AM is a way to see the world from a place of non-judgment; it's an acceptance of what simply is. In this world of apparent duality, we realize that our temporary existence on the planet is an illusionary state, and in fact, at the core of who we truly are, we are eternally one, inseparable source. The practice of I AM reminds us that at the same time we are one with all, we also have the chance to explore different perspectives and create unique contributions in this physical dance of waking life.

A few days before writing this chapter on the I AM Principle of mindfulness, the following words came to me during a morning meditation, and I recorded them in my journal. For me, these words essentially sum up what the I AM Principle encompasses:

Under this skin and these bones, you are unlimited potential—timeless, effortless, and fearless in the name of love. You are creative and expansive, with no limits or gates to pass through when you recognize the essential truth; you no longer stress or strain about fitting in or being accepted by the world around you. This is because you come to realize that you are the world. You are the energy, the source, that is underneath this beating heart in your chest, the source that continually grows your fingernails and hair. You are the source behind every melody sung by the birds and the light streaming down from the sky. You are everything!

Life has no limits. Through the great awareness of I AM, see yourself in a blade of grass, a laughing child, a homeless soul, a thousand-year-old tree. Come to see that this is all you.

The I AM that tends to define you is not the great I AM, for you are everything and nothing all at the same time; you are nothing, in essence, because you are everything. All else is ego and separation. To limit who and what you are is a falsity. It's a miss-take. You live in everything. You are unlimited creativity, ever expanding toward love in all that you do. Everything around you is you. Embrace it all with the eyes of non-judgment and full acceptance, and you will be at peace within and without.

A magical freedom begins to seep into our lives when we are truly willing to release all the attachments that have kept us bound and hostage. When we see past the illusions of "I am what I do for a living," and, "I am what other people think of me," and, "I am what I have acquired," we strip away the layers of egocentric separation and realize, in the spirit of oneness, we are everything, and everything is us. We move into a state of acceptance for all that is, and we mindfully choose to navigate through this temporary world of illusions with a peaceful open heart.

The I AM Exercise

To further demonstrate the principle of I AM, I would like to play a short game with you. I will list several neutralities based on the concept of the neutral I AM. Without overthinking your answers, blurt out or quickly write down how you would fill in the blanks to the following statements:

Work is _____.
This day is _____.
Money is _____.
Love is _____.

My health is _____.
My friends are _____.
The world is _____.
My enemies are _____.
I am _____.

If you did this correctly, without overthinking your responses, I invite you to reflect on what immediately came up for you at the end of each statement. Your impulsive answers most likely represent the pattern running in your unconscious mind. For example, if you answered, money is "hard to come by," you have likely been believing this pattern to be true for you, based on a programmed belief in your unconscious mind. In this statement, money simply is a neutrality: money is. How you chose to fill in the blank about money formulates and/or reveals the pattern in your belief system. Your chosen perspective will determine how you experience money in your life.

If you answered any of these I AM statements in a way you do not want to accept as your reality, you can actually change it right now through applying the principle of I AM to your life. For example, if you filled in the blank for "Money is" with "hard to come by," and don't want to continue believing this to be true, then write a new statement right now. Perhaps, "Money is coming to me from many different sources because money is abundant."

Notice that when you make a perspective change, you may at first deny this new perspective to be true. If this is the case, the inner resistance you're experiencing may be the old pattern, which is threatened by the new perspective you're trying to adopt. As you may recall, our unconscious mind stores all our memory and works to fulfill the requests of our conscious mind. Through consistent repetition, along with feelings of what we deem to be true, we see patterns emerge in our lives.

If we grew up believing that there is not enough money—based on personal experiences and messages we learned from the adults around us—over time, we come to accept this as our reality. Starting today, however, this reality can change—if you want it to. It all begins by realizing you have the power to change the way you think about the neutralities in your life. Money no longer has to be a challenge for you because you can change the way you think about it. Money can start to become a flowing source of joy in your life.

The same goes for any of the statements you wrote down in the exercise. I encourage you to go back over your statements and take time to consciously fill in the blanks with how you would ultimately want to think about these neutralities. As Wayne Dyer powerfully wrote, "When you change the way you look at things, the things you look at change." This becomes a very powerful way to practice the fifth and final principle in the Making Sense of Mindfulness framework: I AM. You can consciously decide how you want your life to unfold. Through the I AM Principle, you choose the way you will experience the neutralities of this world.

CHAPTER 34

THE IMPORTANCE OF FEELINGS AND I AM

The best and most beautiful things in the world cannot be seen or even touched. They must be felt with the heart.
—Helen Keller

can't emphasize enough how important it is to "feel into" your desired intentions. To simply think a thought of abundance will not be enough to attract what you desire. If you truly want a specific outcome to appear, you must not only think it to be true, but you must also *feel* it within all parts of yourself to be true.

Simply thinking you are worthy of love and fully believing it are two different things. If you feel any sort of resistance within your body to the thought of being worthy of love, you will not be able to fully create this reality in your life. For, as we have discovered here, both the mind and body must work together for our higher self to consciously flow through us to deliver what we desire.

If we do not align our thinking and feeling, we will become misaligned and may even get to the point of questioning why things are not the way we want them to be. Pay attention to your thoughts and feelings with extreme intention, knowing you have the ability to think and "feel into" anything you truly want to create in your life. Although what you desire may not instantly appear before you, and it may not even come to you in the original form you were hoping for, know that what you're consciously co-creating with your higher self will be delivered to you in the perfect way and at the perfect time. When we release our mind from overthinking and focus it into the unconscious mind of feelings and beliefs, we will see that what we think we want and what we actually need may be completely different.

A Brand-New Car

Imagine you desire a brand-new car. To truly attract this car into your life, you must align your conscious mind with your unconscious mind. You must not only think about the car and decide you want it, but you must also tap into the feeling of this wish already being fulfilled. There can't be any resistance within your feeling center. If you make a statement such as, "I am the owner of a new car," yet feel resistance within as you speak this out loud, this reality will not likely manifest.

Remember, the only way your higher self can co-create with your conscious mind is through the unconscious mind's feeling center. If you only think about having a new car in your conscious mind, without feeling this to be completely true in your unconscious mind, chances are you will not receive a car in the way you wanted it to flow in. If you only think about a new car, without engaging your feelings to align with your desire, you may only receive an aspect of this desire. For example, you may only receive an advertisement in the mail showing a picture of the car you want.

As you look at the ad, you may not consciously realize it, but the higher self is delivering a brand-new car to you; however, it's not in the form you were hoping for. If it's an actual car you desire, you must "feel into" the actuality of this wish with your physical body and refuse to let resistance or your internal saboteur prevent you from believing in this desire.

You must close your eyes and feel yourself sitting in the new leather seats of the car. You must smell the new-car smell and turn on the radio. You must reach out your hands and grab the steering wheel. You must roll the automatic windows down and open the sunroof. You must see the odometer reading and be so convinced you're driving your new car that you exclaim out loud, "I AM driving my brand-new dream car!" You must believe it to be true on every level of your being. Only then will your higher self be able to deliver you the actual dream car you've been imagining in your consciousness. Our I AM statements must be accompanied by strong, supportive beliefs and feelings of affirmation in order for us to manifest our true desires.

Money Grows on Trees

I was recently conducting a Making Sense of Mindfulness workshop at a local community center for a group of educators who were coming together to learn more about this dynamic practice. As we worked our way through the five-step framework of mindfulness, we arrived at Principle 5: I AM. I had the participants close their eyes and blurt out their current perspectives on the various I AM statements (work is, money is, love is, and so on).

When we reached the end of the exercise, one participant raised her hand and commented that there was no possible way for her to change her relationship with money. She went on to explain that she had struggled her whole life to make ends meet and there was just not enough money in her life to ever get ahead. She made the statement, "Money just doesn't grow on trees, you know. You have to work very hard to make money and to make ends meet." As she spoke, I could hear the frustration in her voice and sensed the Saboteur convincing her she would never get ahead.

I invited her to, once again, close her eyes and imagine standing in front of a tree. Reluctantly, this young woman closed her eyes and envisioned the scene I was inviting her to imagine. I asked her to visualize the tree filled with beautiful leaves of various shades of green. I then had her imagine stepping closer to the tree and noticing that each leaf on the tree was actually a dollar bill. As she visualized this imaginary tree, I asked her how it felt to stand before a money tree with thousands and thousands of dollar bills hanging down before her.

She told me it was a nice idea but not her current reality. I asked her to stay connected to the possibility in her mind and invited her to reach out her hand, pulling a leaf off the tree. As she reached out to grab one of the leaves, I placed a five-dollar bill in her hand. She opened her eyes and tears formed in them. Something was beginning to shift in her awareness. I explained that what we see and feel on the inside is what we will see and experience in the outside world. Our thoughts and feelings will shape how we experience life.

As the woman bought into the possibility that money could literally grow on trees, she received a symbol of money in her hand. Although this was simply a workshop exercise, the new pattern was initiated. She became aware of the old belief she had been carrying and realized it was blocking her from being able to create the reality she desired.

Upon discovering the powerful practice of I AM, this woman began the process of changing her beliefs about money. Since the workshop, she catches herself when speaking and/or thinking the words, "I don't have enough money," with all other forms of this belief, and changes the thought. She consciously monitors her words and feelings to the point where she was recently able to secure a higher paying job, clear up her debt, and put money into her savings account. This is just one of the many miraculous stories that can happen when we apply the principles of mindfulness to our everyday lives. When we truly believe in the power of the I AM Principle, we can create the life we've been imagining.

CHAPTER 35

I AM COMPASSION
AND NON-JUDGMENT

If we have no peace, it is because we have forgotten that we belong to each other.

—Mother Theresa

Are you able to imagine a world where war, racism, prejudice, and violence are nonexistent? What would it truly be like if we were able to drop the stories of separation and fear that play out in our minds, replacing them with stories of love, compassion, and generosity? Imagine news stations that no longer shared the breaking news stories of terrorism, fear, and tragedy. Imagine a world where leaders didn't threaten each other with nuclear warfare, a world where there was equality and acceptance for each and every culture and race. How would this new reality change your experience of life?

As I write this ideal vision for the world, I can feel resistance inside myself. The Saboteur creeps into my mind and yells at me for believing these ideals could be true, telling me a peaceful world does not exist and that people who read this book will roll their eyes at my lofty vision of a harmonious world. Although I still feel inner resistance, I can see the challenge before me: Only when I truly believe (on all levels) that compassion and peace are possible will I experience this reality in my life and in the world.

The practice of mindfulness challenges us to apply its principles to our daily life. As we learn more and more about mindfulness, through the many paths and perspectives of this dynamic practice, one thing remains consistent: All practices of mindfulness will eventually lead us to realizing our inherent connection to oneness, which is the great I AM of Principle 5.

As we become aware of the dynamic practice of I AM, we will see, through the practice of non-judgment and choosing a harmonious perspective, that we have the opportunity to practice compassion in every moment. According to mindfulness teacher and author Susan Kaiser Greenland, compassion is defined as "understanding the suffering of yourself and others, and wanting to help." All of us inherently desire to belong and coexist in harmony. Although our world is filled with examples of imbalance and prejudice, I truly believe these scenarios are of the temporary physical world. Racism, judgment, and violence are simply a forgetting of our true essence. We have become dominated by our overthinking minds and have forgotten that, in essence, we are all connected by one originating source, a source that simply is I AM.

I personally choose to take the perspective that underneath all the suffering, pain, and resistance we experience, an energy connects us all together. This energy is that of eternal oneness. We are all connected. We are all one. But notice, even in a statement such as, "We are all one," I am choosing to believe a certain perspective. The I AM Principle would suggest that it's the "WE ARE" in this statement that represents the most accurate truth in the present moment. We cannot deny that we are.

How I choose to fill in the blank following these two words, "I AM," is going to shape how I experience my life. If I choose to experience life from a place of connectedness and love, I see this truth unfolding all around me. Even if the world appears to be in chaos, I smile inside, knowing that underneath all our subjective perspectives is actually an eternal oneness. When we return to a place of non-judgmental acceptance, we experience neutrality, which binds us all together. It's from this neutral place that we get to explore a mindfulness practice of loving compassion and acceptance.

Nothing Is Wrong with You

I recently delivered a keynote speech at a conference in Northern Canada with several colleagues who were also scheduled to share various messages of motivation to a group of educators. During this trip, I encountered someone that I personally found to be quite irritating. Although I tried my best to practice non-judgment around him, every time this man would speak, I could feel myself becoming more and more agitated by his world views and dominant personality.

I was scheduled to give the closing keynote speech at the event and concluded my presentation by singing a song I had written entitled, "Shine." The theme of this song is remembering how unique and special we are, not letting anyone dim our light. Upon finishing, I had to quickly jump in a taxi and make my way to the airport to fly home with my colleagues.

Just prior to leaving the event, I found myself in conversation with the man who had been irritating me all day and was absolutely taken back by his words. With tears in his eyes, he told me that after hearing my song at the end of the conference, an incredible and profound insight came to him. As he was listening, it dawned on him that many of us live our lives believing something is inherently wrong with one another. He continued to ask, "What would our world be like if we chose to adopt the perspective that there is nothing wrong with each other?"

As I sat there listening to this man share his profound insight, I realized that I, myself, had been holding this belief about him. Without voicing it, I had been internally criticizing him and deeming his way of being in the world as inherently wrong. Although his approach to life was extremely different than mine, instead of accepting him for who he was in that moment, I found myself judging him in my head and writing him off as an egotistical person. As I realized the judgmental perspective I had been holding, I immediately realized my negligence. For in judging this man, I had created a world of separation for myself. I was missing out on profound opportunities to learn and grow from a fellow human being.

Consider how often we criticize and judge each other: "Something seems wrong about her." Imagine what it would be like if we were to practice accepting one another and came from this new perspective instead: "Nothing is wrong with you, and nothing is wrong with me." To see everything around us, including ourselves, as whole, complete, and worthy of love would create a completely different outcome than that produced by prejudice, blame, fear, judgment, and resentment. Although we might not always choose to agree with another's perspective or behavior in the world, what if we could simply practice acceptance and non-judgment, and allow them to be where they are at in their growth and development?

The practice of mindfulness challenges us to practice compassion for ourselves and others. In a mindfulness practice, it's of the utmost importance to monitor our internal thoughts and listen objectively to the words we speak out loud. For in each thought and conversation we engage in, we project into the world our chosen perspective. As we become mindfully aware of the present moment, we can consciously choose only thoughts and words that support a vision of harmony and peace. Although this is a tall order for many of us who are programmed to live our lives in judgment, fear, and separation, the moment we intentionally practice non-judgment and compassion is the moment our world will change. We will come to realize that there is nothing wrong and in fact, in the infinity of life where we are, all is well and perfectly unfolding.

Imagine a World

Imagine a world where elementary school students are taught to love one another and practice compassion on a regular basis, a world where teachers don't see particular students as problem children but instead come from a perspective of "nothing is wrong with you." Can you imagine how it would be if our world leaders decided there was nothing wrong with the opposing forces? How about a shift in perspective surrounding the various religions of the world? What if we allowed everyone to choose their own beliefs without deeming one better or worse than the other? One of my spiritual teachers has always claimed, "Choose what you will but harm none." Imagine what might happen if we truly chose to look at people and our world from a place of non-judgment and acceptance.

Perhaps there would be no need for war, no need to prove one perspective is better than the other. Instead, a stance of loving acceptance would become the norm. Perhaps we would see beyond the color of one's skin and the differences in culture, simply accepting others as beautiful contributors to our planet. Perhaps the violence, rage, and fear would dissipate and we would grow closer together in our inherent ability to love. Perhaps there would be less desire to control, change, manipulate, or judge one another.

Although this may seem farfetched and extremely idealistic, consider that from a place of living in the neutral I AM, these ideals could become reality in your experience. As Gandhi profoundly exclaimed, "[You must] be the change that you wish to see in the world."

Living the I AM Principle

One way to cultivate a practice of I AM and grow your awareness of compassion and acceptance is to live the I AM Principle in your everyday life. No matter where you are, you can practice this as you move throughout your day.

1. To begin, take some time to go for a walk in your current environment. This could be your office, home, or neighborhood—anywhere you are.

2. As you walk, notice the thoughts passing through your mind and notice the various aspects around you that grab your attention. You may see a tree, another person walking, a coworker, or a car.

3. As you tune into the present-moment awareness of your thoughts and observations, monitor the I AM perspective you're choosing. For example, if you come across a coworker in the office, notice what I AM statement crosses your mind. Ask yourself, what perspective am I choosing here? Is this coworker friendly, annoying, in my way, an opportunity to listen, etc.?

4. In each observation, conversation, and/or experience, practice choosing a perspective that accentuates acceptance of what is, without fearfully judging it. Allow everything to be exactly what it is without judgment.

5. Continue this practice as you move through your day. Be aware of when you critically judge or feel that something is not how it should be. Decide if this is the perspective you want to believe in or if a more complimentary perspective would allow you to see the world in a compassionate and non-judgmental way.

"Love On" Exercise

Although many practices of compassion are available, one of my favorite practices was inspired by my good friend Dave. I was recently on a phone call with Dave, and I asked him his plans for the weekend. Dave exclaimed that he was getting together with his family to "love on" his uncle. Upon hearing this, I immediately asked what he meant by "love on" his uncle. Dave explained that his family has a special tradition called "Love On." When it's someone's birthday or somebody has accomplished something great, they come together and "love on" this particular person by cooking him a meal, complimenting him until he blushes, and celebrating his life.

One of the most powerful ways to move into a good state within yourself and to further practice non-judgment and compassion is to share in gratitude with others. From a perspective of gratitude and "loving on," I invite you to find an opportunity each day to share love and compassion. You may choose to write a letter, post a positive blog entry, cook a meal, offer a hug, hold the door open, take the time to listen from a place of non-judgment, or just offer a sincere compliment to someone. To practice coming from a place of appreciation and acceptance is a beautiful way to practice mindfulness in each living moment. Not only will the recipient of your kindness shine brightly, but you, too, will shine brightly. See how many people you can "love on" as you move through your day!

You Are Beautiful

I am currently sitting in a beautiful cabin in the middle of the woods in Northwestern Ontario, Canada. I have been coming to my friend Mark's cabin for several years and have truly enjoyed the amazing connection to nature I experience here. Just last night, as I was writing about mindful compassion, I overheard a phone conversation between Mark and his daughter. My heart broke as I listened to his lovely daughter listing all the things about herself that she disliked. She felt overweight, full of pimples, unattractive, and ugly. I thought about how often we all beat ourselves up with these sabotaging messages, such as "I am ugly"; "I am not good enough"; "I am overweight." So many of us go through life feeling something is inherently wrong with us; negative self-perception has truly become an epidemic. Many times, we don't even realize we're choosing this self-sabotaging perspective or that it's playing out in our thoughts and actions.

As I come to the conclusion of this section on the I AM Principle, I feel compelled to offer an alternative to this negative way of thinking about ourselves. I would like to share a short letter I wrote to the higher self of Mark's daughter in hopes that she will come to realize the power she has to love herself and will acknowledge all the inherent beauty she has. I also dedicate this short letter to all of us, including myself, that we will come to realize how beautiful we truly are and how worthy we are of love and affection:

Dear I AM,

You are the brightest of stars shining in the moonlit sky. You are the most elegant and charming being I have ever seen. You are so worthy of love and affection. Nothing is wrong with you. There has never been anything wrong with you. Perhaps you have had misalignments and learning experiences along the way, but all in all, you are a beautiful miracle on this planet. Do not dim your light. Shine brightly; be proud and true. For you are one of a kind, with no one quite like you.

I urge you, do not give your power away to the naysayers and circus crowd, but instead, stand proudly. You are loveable and worthy. You are enough. You are a unique expression of the divine oneness unfolding on this earth. I see you, and I recognize that you are a beautiful being of love. May you continue to shine infinitely bright, and may you continue to expand into the beautiful, magnificent expression that you are.

Love,

I AM

New Beginnings

One of my favorite excerpts from the Tao Te Ching states the following:

Let yourself be totally empty
Let your mind be at peace
Amidst the rush of worldly coming and going
Notice how endings make way for new beginnings.

Consider that you are not the same person you were when you started reading this book. Even on a cellular level, you have changed. You may have new perspectives, challenges, practices, and wisdom. You may be in a new state of mind, wearing a new set of clothes, and may even be reading these final words in a new location, somewhere else than when you started.

As I reflect on the principles of mindfulness channeled here in this book, I have come to realize that we all have an opportunity to make this practice of mindfulness a new beginning for ourselves every day. Although this is the apparent end of revealing the five steps to living a life of mindfulness, this moment also becomes the beginning of applying and integrating these practices in our everyday lives. With a beginner's mind, we can step out into the world with a whole new way of seeing things. For we can put an end to our ways of being that were not working for us and start anew, applying the five principles found in this text.

Imagine what life will be like when we decide to live our lives from the realization that everything begins as an inner dream: What books will we write? What trips will we take? What imaginings will we dream for ourselves? What relationships will we cultivate?

Beyond this, how will our world unfold when we expose the Saboteur and no longer accept fear as a way of being? Will we have better relationships with ourselves and others? Will we stand tall and proud, honoring the spirit that we are? Will we look in the mirror and see past all the shortcomings our inner critic points out and arrive at a place of loving what we see?

Imagine the possibilities available to us by simply opening our minds and living from a no-limits perspective. Will our breath be more present? Will we fly above all the drama in our life and refuse to participate in limited thinking patterns?

Consider what will take place when we apply the mind-fully aware approach to life. Knowing that our mind and body must work together to create the desired intentions for our life, will we apply the tools we have gained here to manifest our visions into reality? Will we live aligned in mind, body, and higher self, knowing that all three aspects must be cared for and cultivated to experience internal happiness?

As we apply new perspectives to all the ways we look at people and situations, will we now be able to see more clearly what it means to remove judgment? Will we live more compassionately toward ourselves and others as we realize our deepest truth is that of I AM?

As I come to the conclusion of this book, I believe there is an infinite amount of opportunity for us all to grow and implement these powerful principles into our lives. For a life truly committed to practicing these five principles never ceases to learn, expand, and grow. The excitement of what lies ahead for each of us will be greatly influenced by how we decide to apply these five principles to our daily lives:

1. Everything Begins as an Inner Dream
2. Expose the Saboteur

3. Open Your Mind
4. Live Mind-Fully Aware (conscious, unconscious, higher self)
5. I AM

These five steps are the keys to unlocking your life. They are foundational to understanding and navigating through your day-to-day existence. Mindfulness is a way of being in the world, a life-long practice of living a life of awareness and of ensuring that we're implementing intentional action into our lives.

As we come to the end of the formal description of these practices, I urge you to make this a new beginning by stepping out into the world and consciously applying what has resonated for you in these words. For this is truly an opportunity to dream your best dream while you dance through this playground we call life.

I wish you a beautiful continued journey of dreaming your best dream and discovering for yourself what a wonderful and abundant life lies ahead of you as you awaken your abilities to create the life you really want for yourself. "Merrily, merrily, merrily, life is but a dream!" Wake up and consciously dream your best dream!

I leave you with a few words that have channeled through from my higher self onto the page for you.

"The end was just a new beginning. For as all that I knew ceased to be, I awoke to new-found space and once again discovered that in the eternal life, all is one, all is well, and I am safe. I am creation, I am awareness, and I am free."

I love you,

Keith

ABOUT THE AUTHOR

 Keith Macpherson (BEd) is a co-active life coach (The Coaching Training Institute) and motivational speaker who has been inspiring audiences for more than twenty years. Known for his popular "daily intentions" on social media and his regular column "Keith's Corner" in several corporate wellness magazines, Keith inspires thousands of people daily with his messages of mindfulness.

Born and raised in Winnipeg, Manitoba, Canada, Keith has spent much of his life traveling the world as a professional musician with his band, Keith and Renee. In 2006, he was a top finalist on the hit television series *Canadian Idol* and has since released a solo album titled *Shine*.

Aside from music, Keith also is a certified yoga instructor. His instructional videos and *Live Yoga* DVD releases have become increasingly popular along with his live classes across North America. Keith has developed his mindfulness practice amidst the busyness that comes with a career of speaking and performing around the world in markets including the United States, Canada, Mexico, Europe, Dubai, and Africa. His new book, *Making Sense of Mindfulness*, reveals many of the secrets that help him stay in mind, body, and spiritual balance.

Morgan James
Speakers Group

www.TheMorganJamesSpeakersGroup.com

We connect Morgan James published
authors with live and online events
and audiences who will benefit
from their expertise.